JUL 20

P9-CEN-343

the unbeatable Squirrel Girl

THE
ISBN
similar
Printed
Associa
Technol
Comics
1/3/202
10 9 8 7 6

COLLECTION EDITOR: **JENNIFER GRÜNWALD**
ASSISTANT MANAGING EDITOR: **MAIA LOY**
ASSISTANT EDITOR: **CAITLIN O'CONNELL**
EDITOR, SPECIAL PROJECTS: **MARK D. BEAZLEY**
VP PRODUCTION & SPECIAL PROJECTS: **JEFF YOUNGQUIST**
SVP PRINT, SALES & MARKETING: **DAVID GABRIEL**
BOOK DESIGNER: **JAY BOWEN**
EDITOR IN CHIEF: **C.B. CEBULSKI**

BEATABLE SQUIRREL GIRL VOL. 1: SQUIRREL POWER. Contains material originally published in magazine form as THE UNBEATABLE SQUIRREL GIRL #1-4 and MARVEL SUPER-HEROES #8. Fourth printing 2020. 9-0-7851-9702-7. Published by MARVEL WORLDWIDE, INC., a subsidiary of MARVEL ENTERTAINMENT, LLC. OFFICE OF PUBLICATION: 1290 Avenue of the Americas, New York, NY 10104. © 2015 MARVEL No between any of the names, characters, persons, and/or institutions in this magazine with those of any living or dead person or institution is intended, and any such similarity which may exist is purely coincidental. **Canada.** KEVIN FEIGE, Chief Creative Officer; DAN BUCKLEY, President, Marvel Entertainment; JOHN NEE, Publisher; JOE QUESADA, EVP & Creative Director; TOM BREVOORT, SVP of Publishing; DAVID BOGART, Publisher & SVP of Talent Affairs; Publishing & Partnership; DAVID GABRIEL, VP of Print & Digital Publishing; JEFF YOUNGQUIST, VP of Production & Special Projects; DAN CARR, Executive Director of Publishing r; ALEX MORALES, Director of Publishing Operations; DAN EDINGTON, Managing Editor; SUSAN CRESPI, Production Manager; STAN LEE, Chairman Emeritus. For information regarding advertising in Marvel on Marvel.com, please contact Vit DeBellis, Custom Solutions & Integrated Advertising Manager, at vdebellis@marvel.com. For Marvel subscription inquiries, please call 888-511-5480. **Manufactured between nd 1/28/2020 by SOLISCO PRINTERS, SCOTT, QC, CANADA.**

Ryan North
WRITER

Erica Henderson
ARTIST

Maris Wicks (#1), **Kyle Starks** (#3) & **Chris Giarrusso** (#4)
TRADING CARD ART

Rico Renzi
COLOR ARTIST

VC's Clayton Cowles
LETTERER

Erica Henderson
COVER ART

Jon Moisan & Jake Thomas
ASSISTANT EDITORS

Wil Moss
EDITOR

Tom Brevoort
EXECUTIVE EDITOR

SQUIRREL GIRL CREATED BY **WILL MURRAY & STEVE DITKO**

1

Squirrel Girl, Squirrel Girl! She's a human and also squirrel!
Can she climb up a tree? Yes she can, easily.

That's whyyyy
Her name is Squirrel Girl!

Hey, mister! Give us your purse!
Is she tough? Listen bud:
It's not a purse! It's a leather satchel.
She's got partially squirrel blood.

Who's her friend? Don't you know:
That's the squirrel, Tippy-Toe.
Huh? Is she singing?
Is that--is that a tail?

Surprise! She likes to talk to squirrels!
OW!
KA-POW
GAH!

You now have the Spider-Man theme song stuck in your head for the rest of this issue. *You're welcome.*

the unbeatable Squirrel Girl

Words by Ryan North Art by Erica Henderson
Trading Card Art by Maris Wicks
Color Art by Rico Renzi Lettering by VC's Clayton Cowles
Cover by Erica Henderson
Variant Covers by Arthur Adams & Paul Mounts; Siya Oum; Skottie Young

Come on, Tippy-Toe. It's a perfect start to a perfect day, and *I'm* moving into college!

Which means I'm finally moving *out* of the attic of Avengers Mansion--

--also known as my secret apartment--

--and I feel really bad about that so it's a good thing I'm moving out now anyway.

Starring:

Squirrel Girl

a.k.a. DOREEN GREEN

LIKES: squirrels (luckily)
DISLIKES: **injustice**
FUN FACT: is a woman with the proportional speed and strength of a squirrel!

Tippy-Toe

a.k.a. TIP a.k.a. TIPPY a.k.a. T-TOE

LIKES: nuts
DISLIKES: not nuts
FUN FACT: is a squirrel with the proportional speed and strength of a squirrel!

Park Muggers

a.k.a. WE ALREADY BEAT THEM UP

LIKES: free money
DISLIKES: free punches
FUN FACT: they all just learned the error of their ways via punches!

?

a.k.a. WE HAVEN'T MET HIM YET

LIKES: ?
DISLIKES: ??
FUN FACT: ?!?!?!??

Wait, did I say the Spider-Man theme song? *Obviously* I meant the *Squirrel Girl* theme song. Who even *is* Spider-Man?

NOT PICTURED: Other tiny boxes labelled "Ant-Man's Tiny Vans," "Ant-Man's Aunt's Flans," and "Ant-Man's Rejected Costumes (OFF-Brand)"

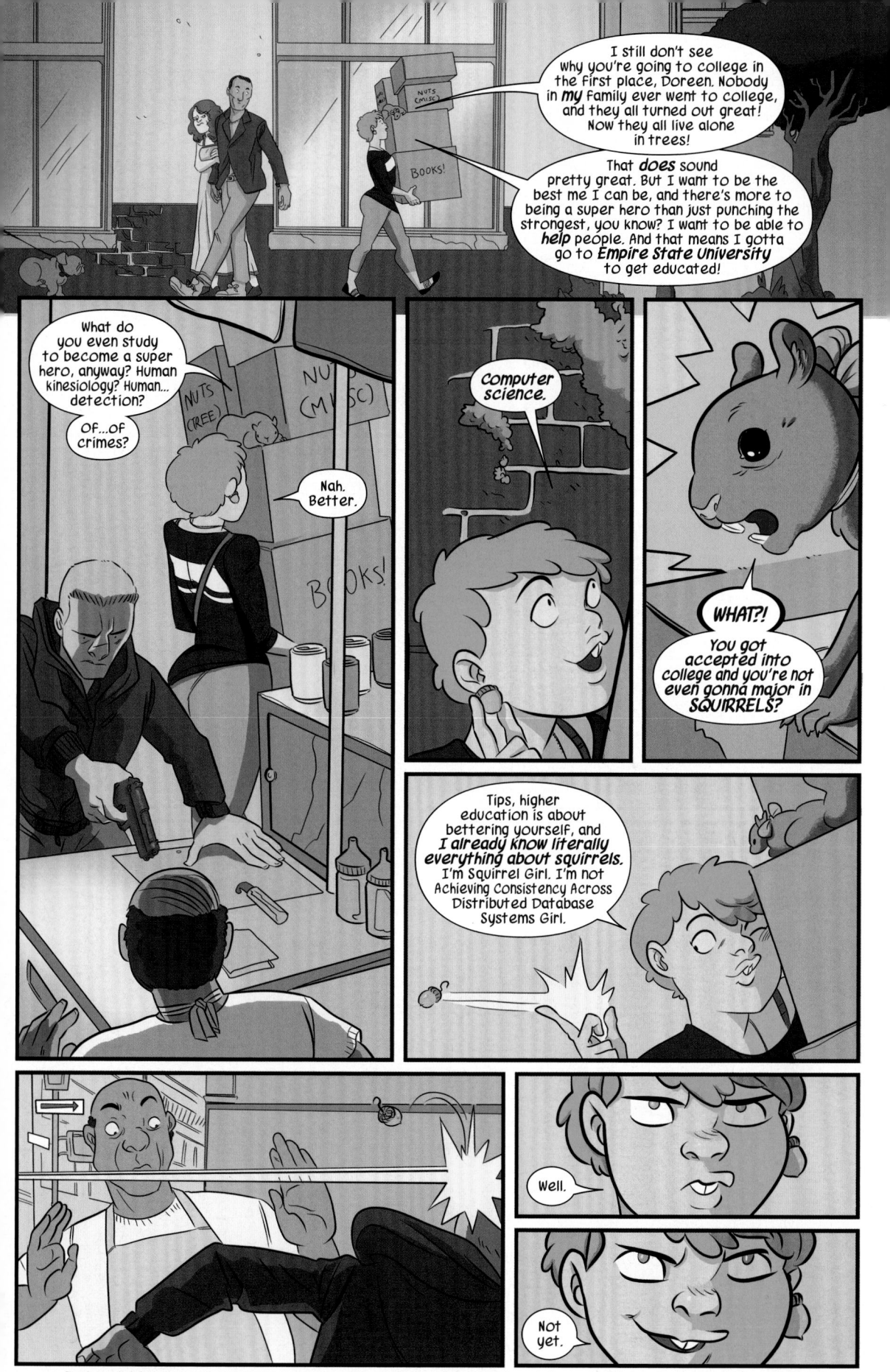

There's more to being a super hero than just being the strongest! For example, you might also be the fastest, or the smartest, or have the ability to breathe in space like it isn't even a big deal.

Also, my name rhymes. Yes, that too is but one of the ***several*** ways in which I am totally regular.

I'm, uh, just moving all these empty boxes into my dorm, and that way I'll be ready to help when it's time to move out of the dorms!

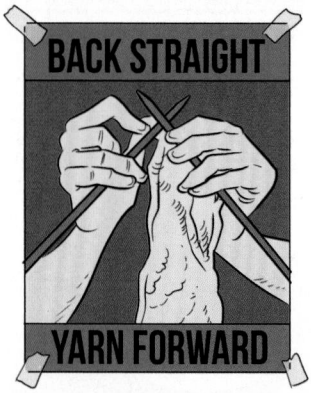

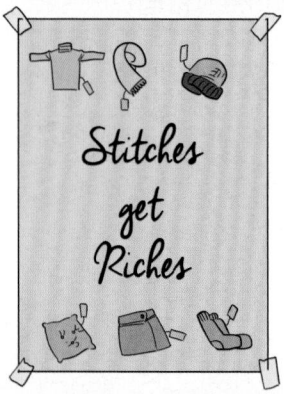

DID YOU KNOW: Mew is named after "Mewnir," which is the name of Cat Thor's hammer? DID YOU ALSO KNOW: Cat Thor is a character in Nancy's Fan Fiction, "Cat Thor: Cat God of Cat Thunder"??

DID YOU KNOW: college administrator was the job Kraven the Hunter was training for before he took a chance weekend safari getaway? Yes! It's almost possibly a fact!

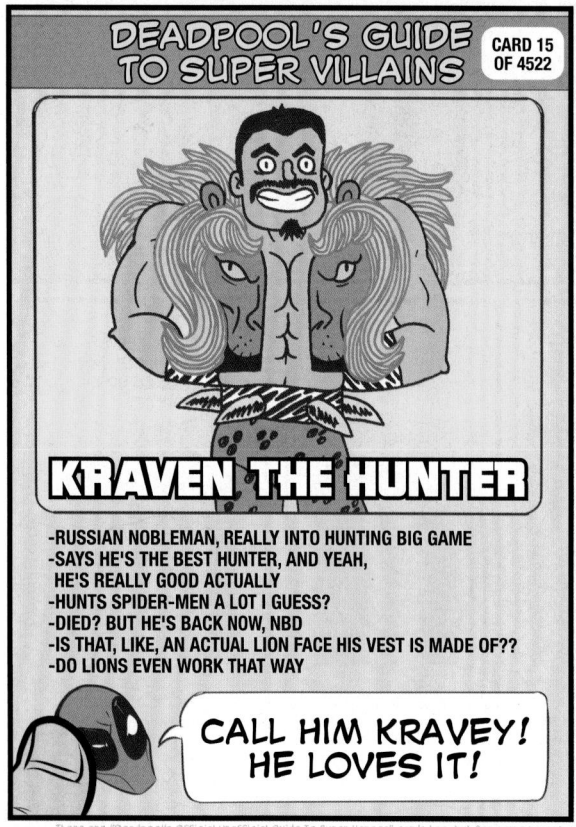

There are "Deadpool's Official unOfficial Guide To Super Heroes" cards too, but for some reason every pack is like 99% pictures of Deadpool looking at himself in a mirror and giving himself a thumbs up.

Listen, all I have are these "Deadpool Super Villain" cards, not "Deadpool Great One-Liners For Heroes To Use On Super Villain" cards. I'm not made of money over here.

In retrospect, the song *does* spend a surprisingly large percentage of its time describing my friends, my favourite foods, and where I like to hang out. Hindsight's always 20/20, huh?

Congratulations to "LET'S GET NUTS" for beating out runners-up "LET'S GET CRAZY" and "LET'S BECOME ECCENTRIC" in the What Should Squirrel Girl Say When Biting Her Way Out Of A Net Competition, 2015

Another runner-up was "LET'S GO BANANAS," before that phrase was disqualified for also having competed in the What Should Man-Ape Say When Biting Into A Banana Really Intensely Competition, 2015.

Squirrels in pants? Squirrels...*eating* pants? *Squirrels secretly replacing pants with other squirrels??*

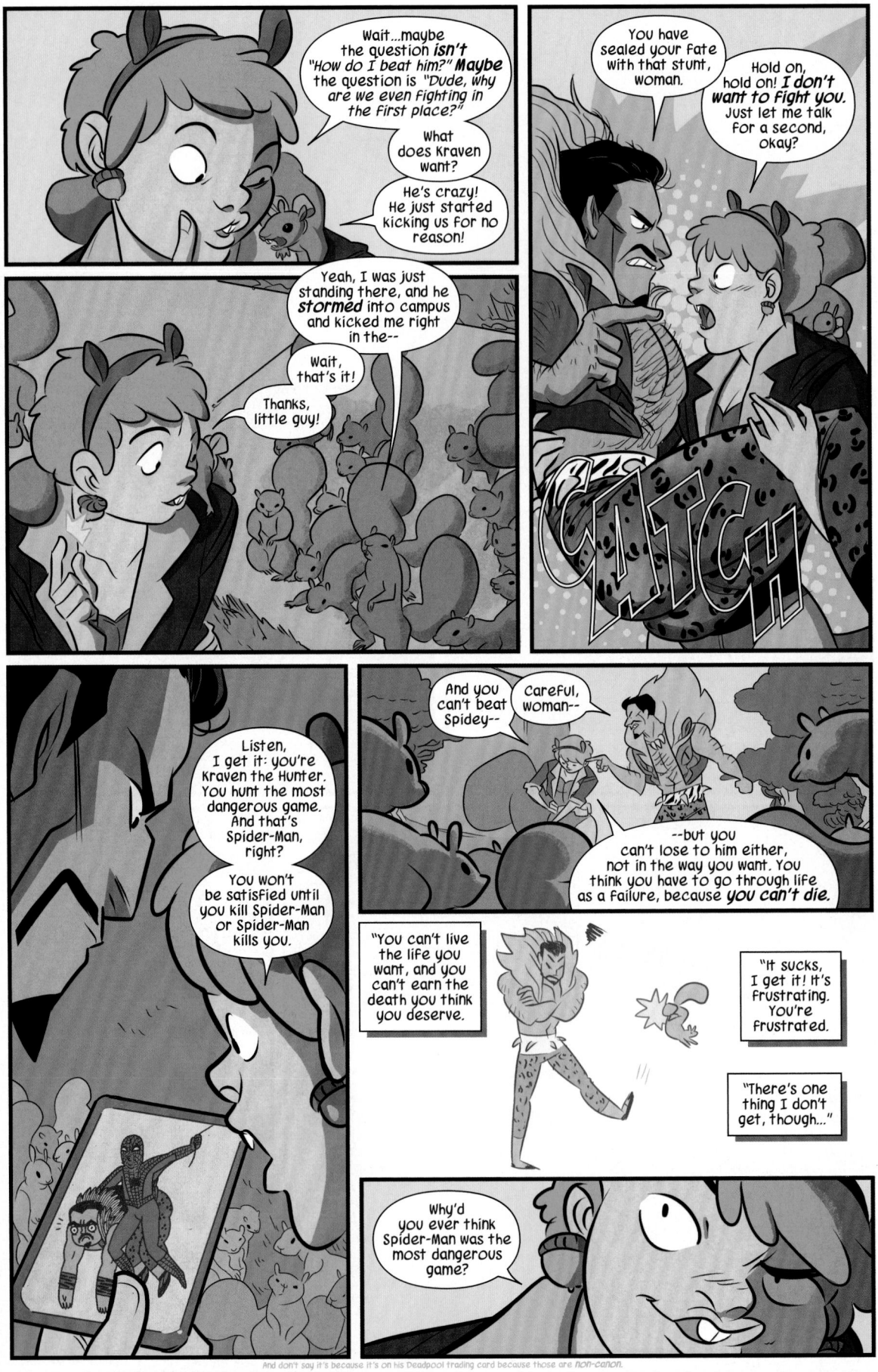

And don't say it's because it's on his Deadpool trading card because those are non-canon.

If you *think* there's someone who goes here and who looks like me then my only comment on that matter is *"okay wow she sounds hot!"*

Also, sad I guess. Sad and cheesed. It's--it's a really familiar feeling?

Those of you who *can* speak Northeastern variant Squirrelese are freaking out right now, but don't tell anyone! Keep it a surprise for the rest of us who have to read the next page to find out what the deal is, okay?

Nancy, would you excuse us for a moment?

Come on, Tippy. I'm pretty sure the entire planet isn't totally doomed.
It is! Something colossal is headed towards Earth, Doreen! The Squirrel Information Network has reports from squirrels around the world of stars being blocked out!

Calm down. Hey, since when do squirrels stargaze? And from where?
Forest observatories, obviously.
Guess there's still some stuff you have left to learn about squirrels after all, huh?

Seriously though, Doreen: whatever it is, it's colossal and it's headed here and it's not stopping. It's up to us to save the planet!
How much time have we got?
I dunno. I mean, it's millions and millions of miles out in space, so you know: definitely a while. Still!

Well, what are you worried about then, you big baby? Space is huge and we've got plenty of time to figure this out. Come on, let's go to orientation. After all...
...What's the worst that could happen?

Coming next issue...
...the worst that could happen!

Letters From Nuts

Ryan!

Erica!

Send letters to mheroes@marvel.com or 135 W 50th St. 7th Floor, New York, NY 10020 (Please mark "OKAY TO PRINT")

Hello! We're Erica and Ryan and Rico, we're writing and drawing and coloring a comic about a woman with squirrel powers. We've actually been writing and drawing and coloring this comic for YEARS, decades really, and last month Marvel came to us and asked if they could publish it, and we said "YES!" and then went on to say "Also we've been kinda using your character so you don't really have to ask, also thanks for not suing us."

OKAY NO that's nut true. We only started this comic recently! But we ARE following in the footsteps of the people who have made Squirrel Girl comics before: great guys like Will Murray, Steve Ditko, Dan Slott, Paul Pelletier, Brian Michael Bendis and Mike Deodato!

This book is an experiment: can a book like this find an audience? Will people TRULY read a comic about someone who dresses up like a rodent-like animal and fights crime in a major metropolitan area, even if that animal ISN'T a bat?? We hope they will. If you liked this comic, share it! Tell your friends! Tell the WHOLE WORLD you liked it, because then they might like it too, and then we'll all get more comics like this: fun, funny, awesome books about a crime-fighter with a utility belt and animal-themed gadgets (again, NOT a bat). And if you've got a computer, you can check out unbeatablesquirrelgirl.tumblr.com where we post SNEAK PEEKS at upcoming issues and behind-the-scenes art!

We thought we'd start here with your letters. You can send them to MHEROES@MARVEL.COM, and don't forget to mark them "OKAY TO PRINT" so we know your letter is cool to print. But since this is our first issue all we've gotten so far are some TOTALLY FAKE LETTERS we'll use to get the ball rolling! Can YOU send us something better? I'd sincerely like to see that!!

Q: Excuse me, but how are you following me, how are you getting all this information??

- D. Green

A: Erica is really good at sketching quickly AND at being discreet. A winning combination!

Q: Who wrote Squirrel Girl's theme song?

- Pat W.

A: The song was composed by Academy Award winner Paul Francis Webster and Robert "Bob" Harris in 1967, but at the time it was accidentally applied to another obscure Marvel character named "Spider-Man." Several decades later we detected this error and corrected it, restoring the song to its originally intended glory, and now it's totally about a woman who talks to squirrels.

Q: Who would win in a fight, Squirrel Girl or the Hulk?

- Jenn K.

A: If you ask the Hulk team, they might say something different, which is frankly ADORABLE, but clearly it's Squirrel Girl. Is their character called "The Unbeatable Hulk"? No, they call him "The Incredible Hulk," as in "Incredible! The Hulk just got beat up by Squirrel Girl, she's the greatest and I love her forever!!"

Q: Who would win in a fight, Squirrel Girl or Ms. Marvel?

- Emily H.

A: Yo, why are they fighting? Doreen and Kamala are on the same side here, so it's LITERALLY CRAZY that they're fighting. A better question is who would Squirrel Girl and Ms. Marvel fight FIRST?? My money is on EVERYONE WHO STANDS IN THEIR WAY.

Q: Who would win in a fight, Tippy-Toe the Squirrel or Howard the Duck?

- Chip Z.

A: Tippy-Toe is a regular squirrel with zero super powers, and Howard the Duck is a sentient duck who is approximately as smart as the average human! That said, Tippy-Toe. PROVE ME WRONG, HOWARD.

Q: Who would YOU rather fight, one squirrel-sized Hulk or a hundred Hulk-sized squirrels?

- Lucy W.

A: Doreen would obviously take the squirrel-sized Hulk, seeing as she'd never want to fight squirrels since they are ULTIMATE PALS. Personally, I'd take the squirrel-sized Hulk too, because while I wouldn't like the Hulk when he's angry, I would LOVE him when ADORABLY-SIZED, super-cute, and could fit inside a bottle of pop.

I don't know why I apparently keep trying to pick a fight with the Hulk team here. Send us some letters! DO IT!!

Thanks everyone, and we'll see you next month!

When you see this: AR, open up the MARVEL AR APP (available on applicable Apple ® iOS or Android ™ devices) and use your camera-enabled device to unlock extra-special exclusive features!

2
EH!

Should we say you'll find him deep within the...interGALACTUS stellar medium?? We shouldn't? Oh. Okay.

The next five rules of Mew Club are to tell everyone about Mew Club; we need members really badly

Not pictured: Way Too Lazy To Set Up A Booth Club

Hey, did you know you can give yourself tattoos at home? It's true! ***But don't tell any authority figures I told you,*** I don't want to get in trouble

Here we are in issue 2 already summarizing what happened in issue 1! It's fine for now, but at a certain point I'm gonna have to stop these summaries and you'll just have to buy the comics to find out what happened, okay??

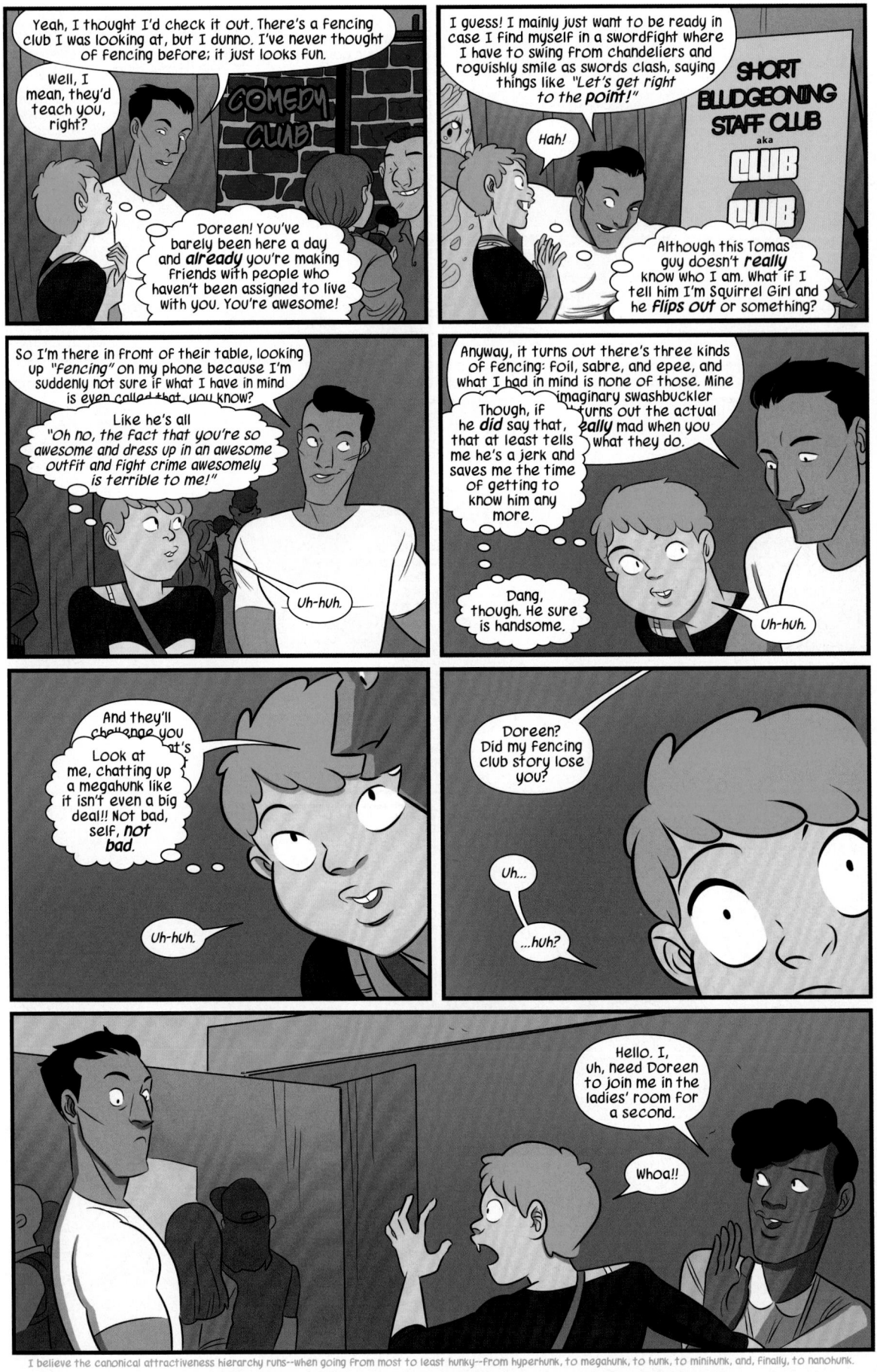

I believe the canonical attractiveness hierarchy runs--when going from most to least hunky--from hyperhunk, to megahunk, to hunk, to minihunk, and, finally, to nanohunk.

Hello, I'm the new exchange student, Sally Awesomelegs. This is my real name and definitely not a secret identity I just made up in the bathroom while looking at my legs.

Yes, Tippy-Toe did absolutely start this page imagining that window would dramatically smash around her as she leapt through it.

Honestly I wish there was time to do both, but there's not, and a girl has to make choices sometimes. Someone else join anime club for me, I'll catch up later.

People who make fun of selfies always act like they wouldn't take a selfie after they defeated Galactus. People who make fun of selfies are *dang liars.*

NYC cab insurance has a small deductible for super hero footprint damage. Don't worry about it!

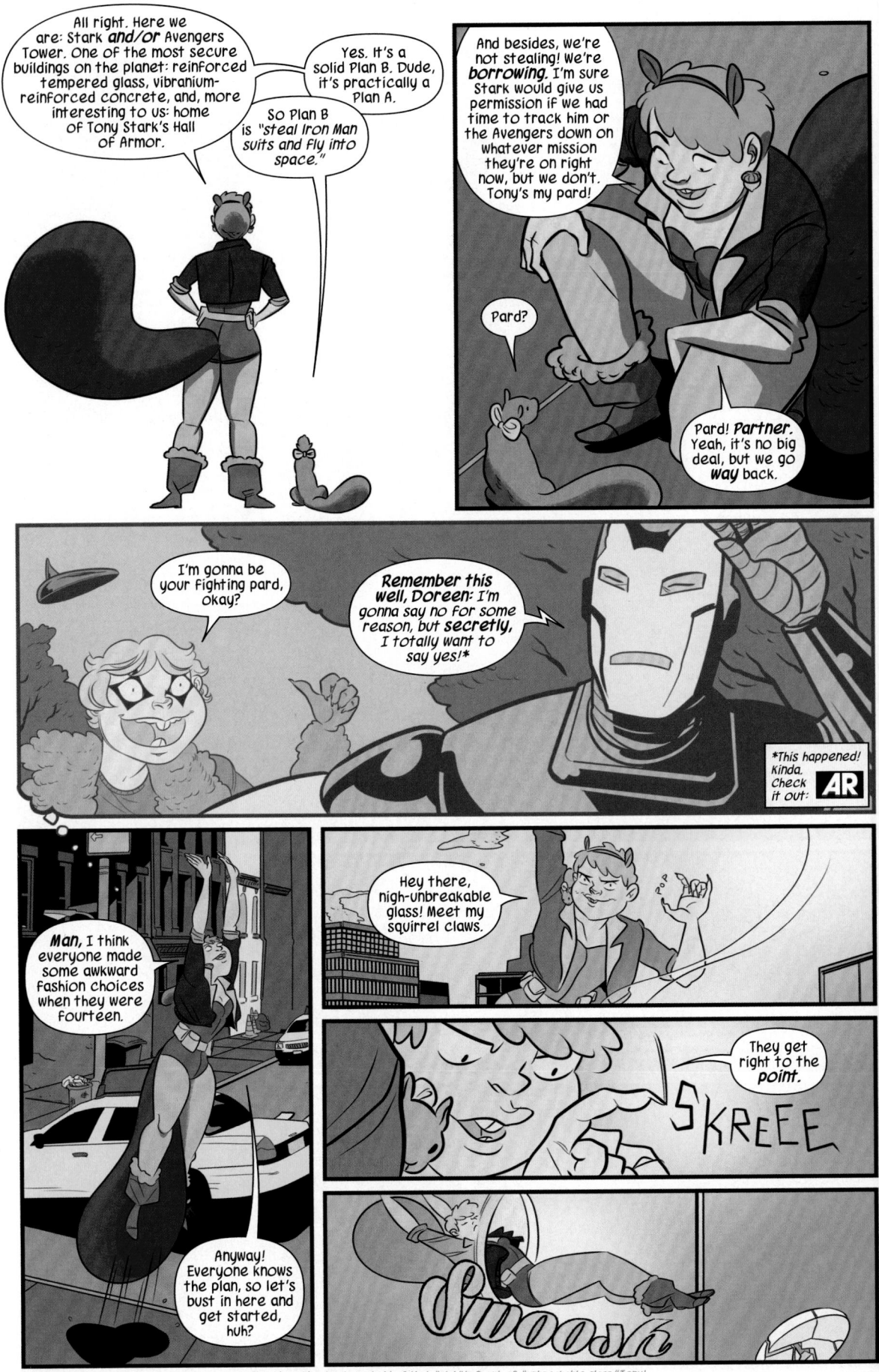

Shoulda paid extra to get rid of that "nigh" in front of "unbreakable glass," Tony!

Okay, now breathe through your mouth! That way we can still taste them, so we're not wasting these delicious nuts.

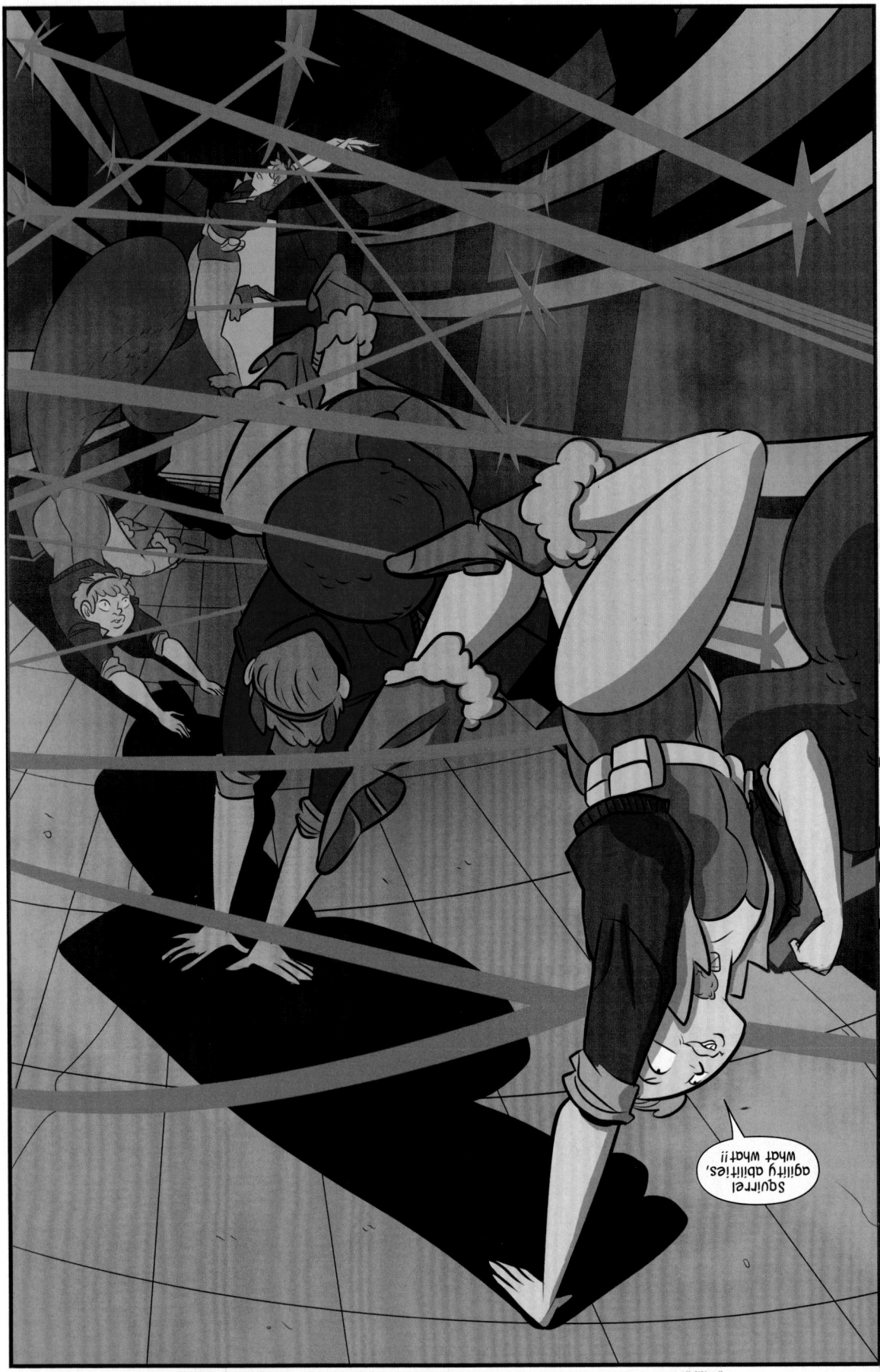

As my Aunt Benjamina used to say, "With great squirrel agility ability comes great squirrel agility responsibility."

All I'm saying is, if these Iron Man robots are anything like my phone, then they cost way too much and don't work very well after you drop them in the toilet.

That "PHWEEEEEeeee" is the sound of the repulsors charging up. The robots aren't saying the "PHWEEEEEeeee" noises themselves, although that would've been *kinda adorable.*

I didn't let you, the reader, know her plan before now because it's a better narrative surprise this way! *Also:* how do I know I can trust you, huh?? You could be *literally anyone.*

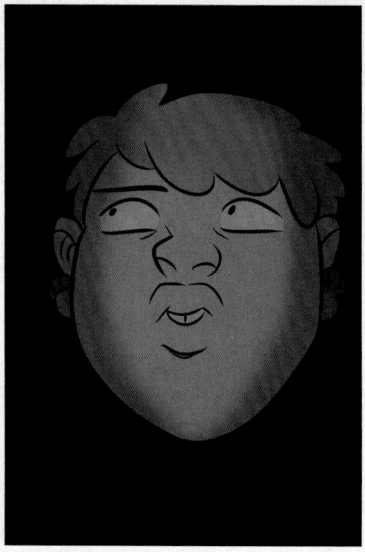

BODY TYPE: Rad / TAIL TYPE: Unexpected / CLAW TYPE: Geez, Tony, you really need to get these nails under control.

We choose to go to the Friggin' moon! We choose to go to the Friggin' moon in these suits and do the other things, not because they is easy, but because they are awesome. Also, if we don't, the planet will get eaten. So, lots of reasons, really.

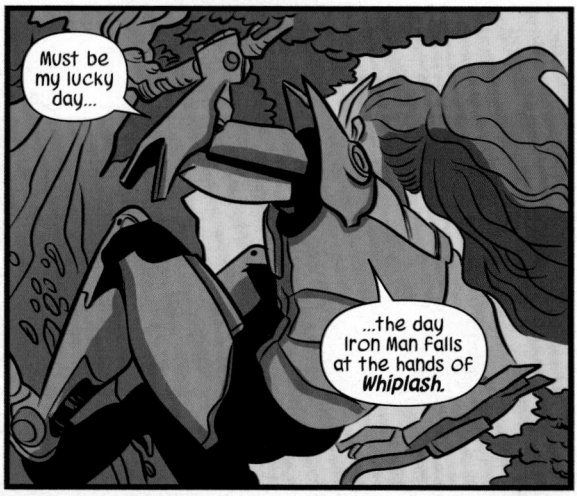

Next month: *Galactus* and *Whiplash* vs *a woman in a robot suit she borrowed.*

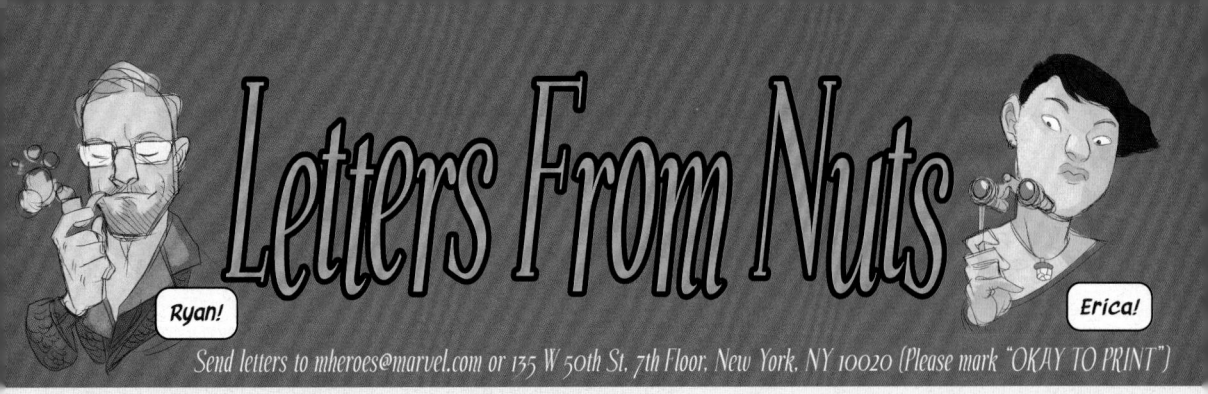

Send letters to mheroes@marvel.com or 135 W 50th St. 7th Floor, New York, NY 10020 (Please mark "OKAY TO PRINT")

Last month we said all the letters were fake because you hadn't sent us any yet, but now we have TONS and all the letters are real! We love to hear from you: send your email to MHEROES@MARVEL.COM, and don't forget to mark "OKAY TO PRINT" in there somewhere. And be sure to follow our production blog at unbeatablesquirrelgirl.tumblr.com! We post fan art, sneak peeks, sketches, recordings of Squirrel Girl's theme song we made in our kitchens - all sorts of fun stuff!

YOUR LETTERS:

Q: In issue #1's letters you wrote, "Can a book like this find an audience?" We live in a post-Superior Foes of Spider-Man world; more and more we readers like having the "comic" in our comics. You've found an audience in this guy, that's for sure! Was it Ryan/Erica or the editors who wrote the subscript footnotes? Because that was NUT a bad idea. I hope the footnotes are a continued part of the comic mag!

- Trent H.

A: Yeah, that was me (Ryan) doing that! I like the idea of secrets that you get to discover when you read a comic, and I really hope there are people who only noticed those secret words halfway through (or perhaps, just now, as they're reading this, and now they're going back to see what they missed?). They will continue forever because I love writing them forever!

Q: Squirrels. Cannot. Give. You. RABIES!!! Look it up!! Doreen would have known this and corrected her new roommate (even if she didn't know about the squirrel observatories).

-Benjamin G.
True Squirrel Fan

A: ATTENTION EVERYONE: I looked into this and BENJAMIN IS CORRECT. Squirrels don't even normally GET rabies, because to get it they'd have to hang around with animals that typically carry it, and most of those animals try to eat all the squirrels they see. Squirrel bites are apparently one of the few animal bites that don't trigger a hospital vaccination protocol! GOOD TO KNOW.

PS: if you get bitten by a squirrel, maaaaybe still check with a doctor just in case? You know, before you take the medical advice you found in the letters page of a comic book.

ERICA: I have personal experience with this, actually. As a young teenager, I think you call them tweens now, during the time when most Marvel characters gain their superhuman abilities, I was bitten by a squirrel. I was tested, but did not get rabies. We did not test for radiation. It might have been a radioactive squirrel. If you ask, I'll show you my scar.

Q: Thank you, Erica, for drawing Squirrel Girl not like a sex symbol (I feel awkward when I discovered about she and Logan...). And thank you, Ryan, for showing us that Squirrel Girl is a geek too. It's good to read comics about a girl who is a fan of comics too, and a little tomboy (I'm a tomboy girl too).

Will we see romance between Speedball and Squirrel Girl? I know we are gonna see a lot of Marvel stars in this comic. But I hope to see those love birds together again.

- ScarlettShana

A: Aw, thanks! I wouldn't worry about that Wolverine thing though: all we knew for SURE is that she and Wolverine at one point agreed to never see each other again. BUT NOW I CAN TELL YOU WHY: several years ago, Doreen was about to get into a cab when Wolverine ran up and hopped inside, stealing it from her. Squirrel Girl was (understandably) SUPER-CHEESED and shouted that he was a jerk and his jerkiness must have its OWN healing factor and that she never wanted to see him again. As the cab drove off Wolverine rolled down the window and shouted "You too, bub!". And that's why things were awkward when they met again! THE END.

As for romance with Speedball, everyone has a little romance in their lives at some point, right? But I have a feeling Doreen might have feelings for someone new now...

ERICA: You're welcome, but honestly I just drew her the way I saw her and I don't see her as a sexy character. She's not exactly Emma Frost, you know?

Q: Does Doreen have a flying squirrel costume that opens up and lets her glide?

- Simon S.

A: SPOILER ALERT (IF YOU'RE READING THIS COMIC FROM BACK TO FRONT, THAT IS): She gets an Iron Squirrel outfit this issue, so - kinda! But a base-jumping suit would be PRETTY AMAZING for her to get down the road.

ERICA: Well, I know that S.H.I.E.L.D. has had base-jumping suits for decades and Dum Dum Dugan did invite Doreen to join S.H.I.E.L.D. at one point, so she might have access to some later...

Q: First off, I have to say how absolutely MARVELous (ha!) the first issue of Unbeatable Squirrel Girl was! Wow! Artwork and writing combined, it's pretty much the most perfect comic book of all time and space. Secondly, I have to say how super AWESOME it is to have another female-fronted book, but also one where the character is hilarious and clumsy and endearing and basically a lot more like me than any of the other beautiful, graceful super-women out there. (I love them too, though!) I love everything you've done and I absolutely canNUT wait for the next issue! (One day I'll stop with the puns. Today is NUT that day.)

- Holly R.

A: Thank you! One thing both Erica and I discovered while making this book is how often every day (without thinking!) we would say something is "nuts" or "nutty" or how we'd like "acorn" ("a corn") for dinner. The puns come almost TOO easily!

ERICA: My main thing is I like to draw heartier super ladies, if their powers are mostly physical, because I feel like I shouldn't be able to take down a super hero by sitting on her.

Q: Is it true Squirrel Girl would've been in Avengers 2, but Ultron was too chicken to fight her?

- Andy D.

A: That movie isn't even out yet! How do you know she's NOT in it?? ...But on the off chance that for some reason she isn't, yeah, probably that's the reason! I'm guessing the after-credits scene is just Ultron peeking around corners to make sure Squirrel Girl isn't there, then wiping his forehead and saying "PHEW! CLOSE CALL."

ERICA: I don't know about that, but they need to add her to the movies soon because who's going to take down Thanos???

That's all we have room for, but look for a double-sized letters page next issue! See y'all next month! Stay nutty!

When you see this: AR, open up the MARVEL AR APP (available on applicable Apple ® iOS or Android ™ devices) and use your camera-enabled device to unlock extra-special exclusive features!

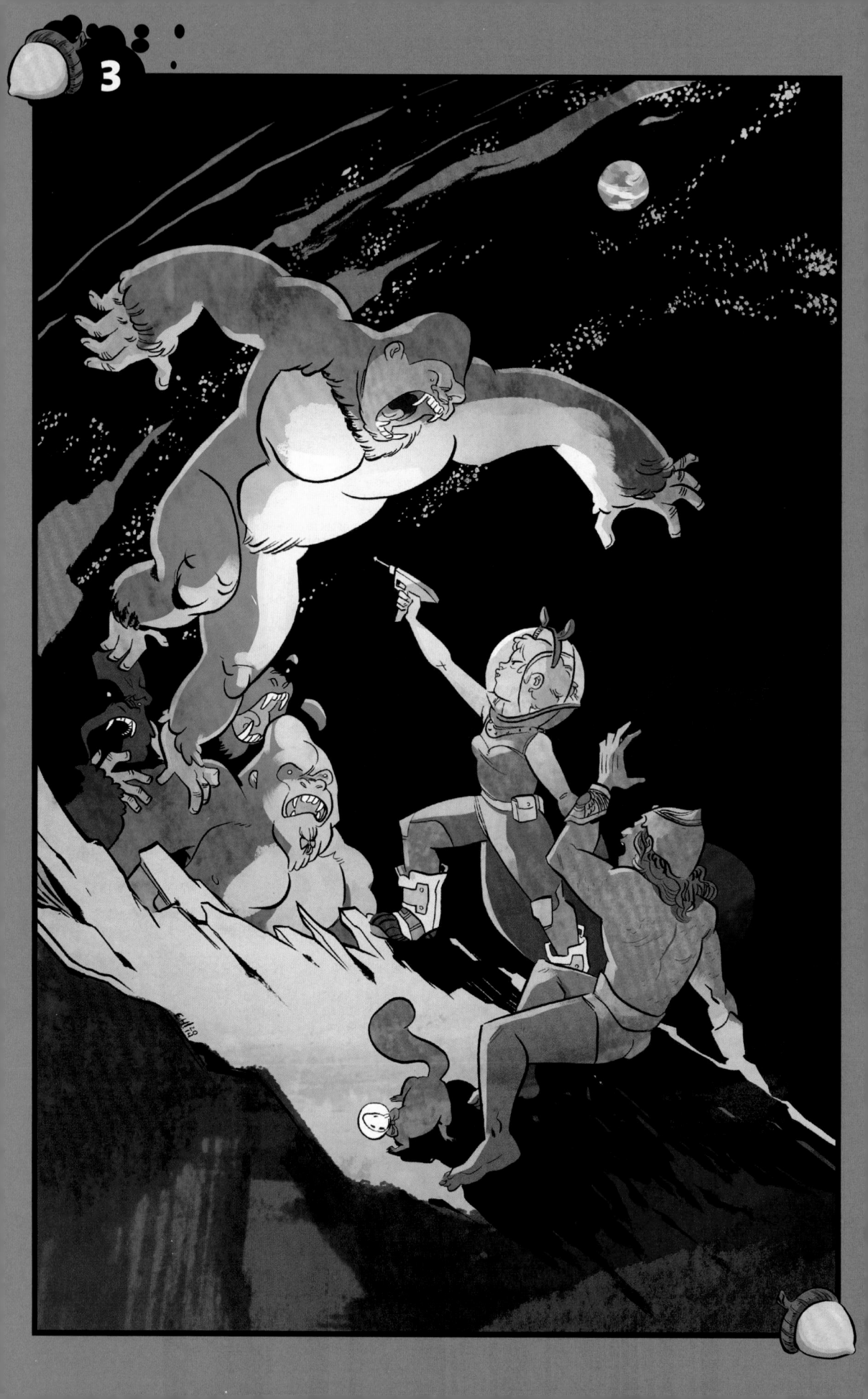
3

Doreen Green isn't just a first-year computer science student: she secretly also has all the powers of both squirrel and girl! She uses her amazing abilities to fight crime **and** be as awesome as possible. You know her as...**The Unbeatable Squirrel Girl!** Let's catch up with what she's been up to until now, with...

Squirrel Girl *in a nutshell*

Squirrel Girl! @unbeatablesg
Did you guys see how I took care of Kraven the other day?

xKravenTheHunterx @unshavenkraven
NOBODY LISTEN TO @unbeatablesg, SHE DIDN'T TAKE CARE OF ME, I MERELY DECIDED TO STOP FIGHTING HER

Squirrel Girl! @unbeatablesg
@unshavenkraven hey dude did you kill any gigantos underwater like I suggested?

xKravenTheHunterx @unshavenkraven
@unbeatablesg listen

xKravenTheHunterx @unshavenkraven
@unbeatablesg these things take time

Squirrel Girl! @unbeatablesg
Apparently I'm the only one that can see that GALACTUS IS COMING TO EARTH!!

Tippy-Toe @yoitstippytoe
CHIT CHUKKA CHITTY

Squirrel Girl! @unbeatablesg
Apparently me and @yoitstippytoe are the only ones that can see GALACTUS IS COMING TO EARTH!!

Squirrel Girl! @unbeatablesg
Oh well

Squirrel Girl! @unbeatablesg
guess we'll just have to stop him ourselves then

Squirrel Girl! @unbeatablesg
ON THE FRIGGIN' MOON

Tony Stark @starkmantony
Whoever "borrowed" Iron Man armor parts from my NYC offices, please return them. Looking at you, @unbeatablesg.

Squirrel Girl! @unbeatablesg
@starkmantony Tony it's REALLY IMPORTANT. Like COSMIC important.

Squirrel Girl! @unbeatablesg
@starkmantony I don't know why I'm being coy. It's for Galactus.

Squirrel Girl! @unbeatablesg
@starkmantony I'm gonna beat up @xGALACTUSx, Tony!! ON THE MOON

Tony Stark @starkmantony
@unbeatablesg You break it, you bought it.

Whiplash @realwhiplash22
I JUST WHIPPED @STARKMANTONY OUT OF THE SKY WITH MY ENERGY WHIPS YES YES #OWNED

Tony Stark @starkmantony
Wasn't me. I'm in San Francisco, @realwhiplash22.

Whiplash @realwhiplash22
@starkmantony SORRY I CANNOT HEAR YOU OVER HOW BADLY YOU GOT #OWNED

search!

- #OWNED
- #everythingisnormalinspace
- Welcome to
- #USG
- Number Three
- Hope you like falafel jokes

If you want to stop reading this comic to go get some Falafel, I understand. In fact, I might join you!

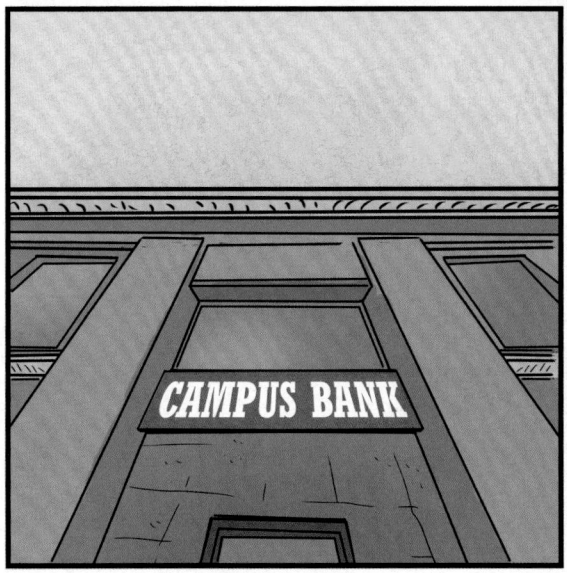

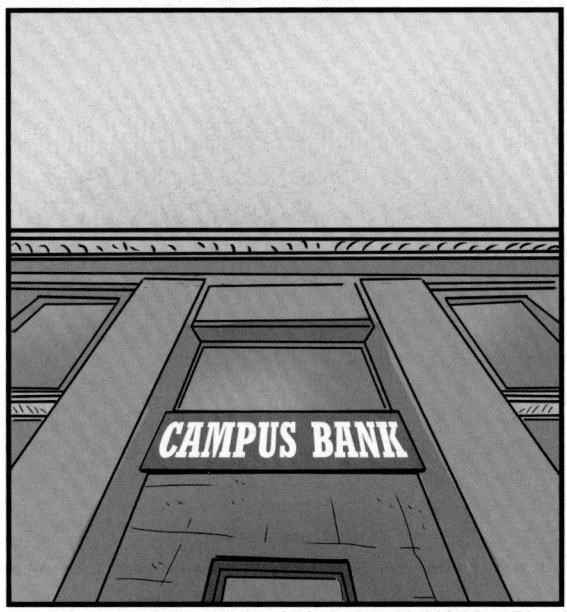

Dang, you guys, these falafel I got are friggin' delicious!! This is why comics are the best: you can pause at any time to go eat falafel, so check and mate, ***all other media.*** Except books, I guess. ***Fine,*** books are good, too.

Okay, real talk: if you look it up online, you'll find Galactus's *actual* name is "Galan." I'm not joking, it's Galan. Galan A. Lactus.

Wait, this makes two Russian nationals that Doreen has faced off against in as many issues! Looks like these comic issues have their *own* not-so-comic issues, am I right??

Excuse me, but I'm "Whiplash." "Whip-Man" is just an annoying friend of mine with some cheap knock-off of my very expensive technowhips.

This isn't actual American Sign Language, but if you can think of a better hand symbol for "Galactus" then I'm, *um,* all ears.

You know what happens to a squirrel when it gets mad? *The same thing that happens to everything else.* Which is to say, increased heart rate, elevated adrenaline and norepinephrine production, a lessened capacity for self-monitoring, etc., etc.

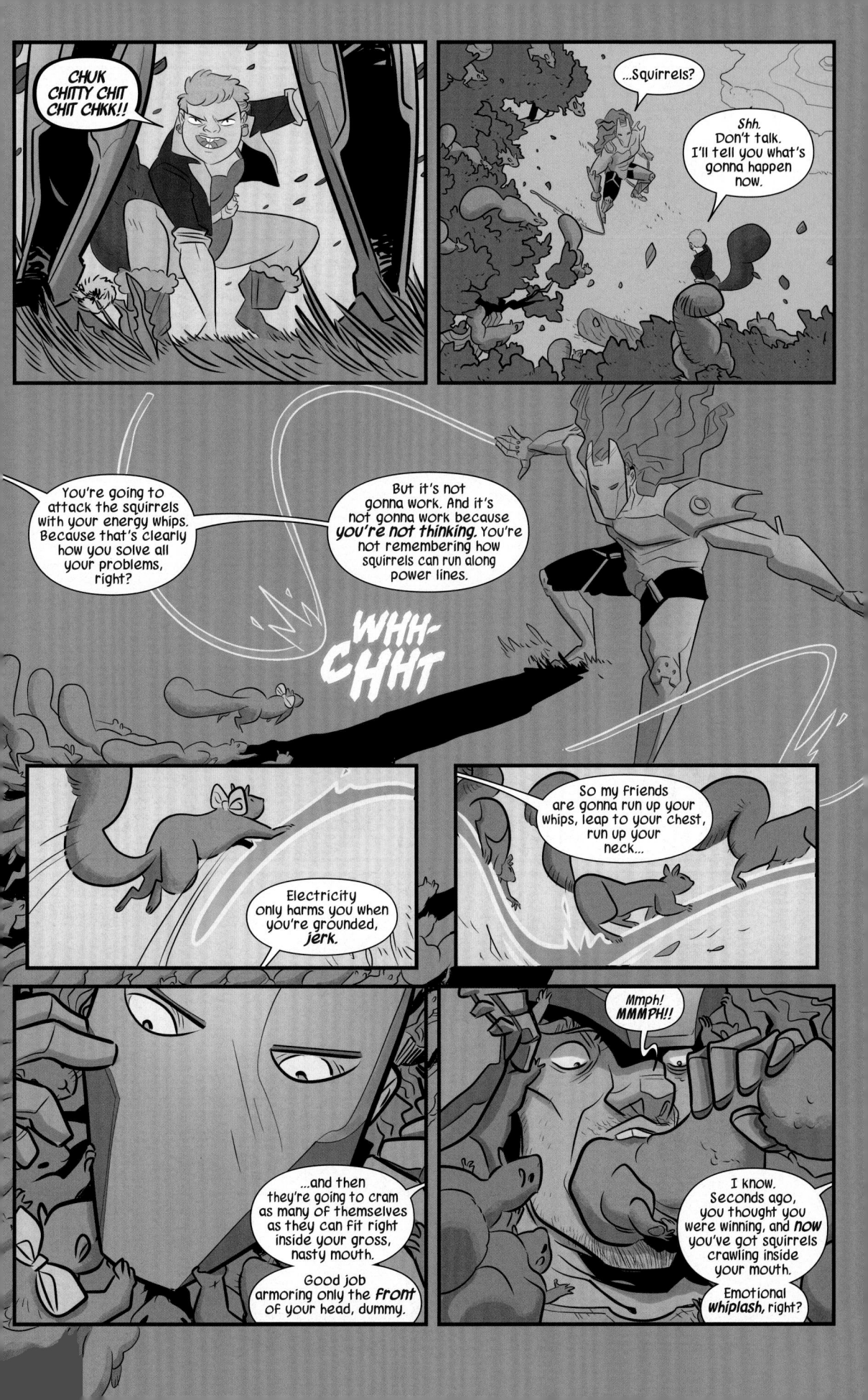
CHUK CHITTY CHIT CHIT CHKK!!
...Squirrels?
Shh. Don't talk. I'll tell you what's gonna happen now.
You're going to attack the squirrels with your energy whips. Because that's clearly how you solve all your problems, right?
But it's not gonna work. And it's not gonna work because you're not thinking. You're not remembering how squirrels can run along power lines.
WHH-CHHT
Electricity only harms you when you're grounded, jerk.
So my friends are gonna run up your whips, leap to your chest, run up your neck...
...and then they're going to cram as many of themselves as they can fit right inside your gross, nasty mouth.
Good job armoring only the front of your head, dummy.
Mmph! MMMPH!!
I know. Seconds ago, you thought you were winning, and now you've got squirrels crawling inside your mouth.
Emotional whiplash, right?

Chipmunk Hunk, Chipmunk Hunk / He fights crime and other junk / Is he great? Listen punk: Something something something unk

To hiiiiim, he is a great big chipmunk / Wherever there's some street punks / You'll find the Chipmunk Hunk!

All right, sorry, I just got excited about Chipmunk Hunk.
Back to Squirrel Girl, huh? But she's not even on this page. *Sheesh!*

Attention, all units: be on the lookout for sucky Larrys in the area. Subjects are to be considered potentially armed and definitely sucky.

In retrospect, Wikipedia *did* mention that groups of squirrels could combine to form giant squirrel-based objects, but I just assumed it was vandalism. I was a fool. A fool!!

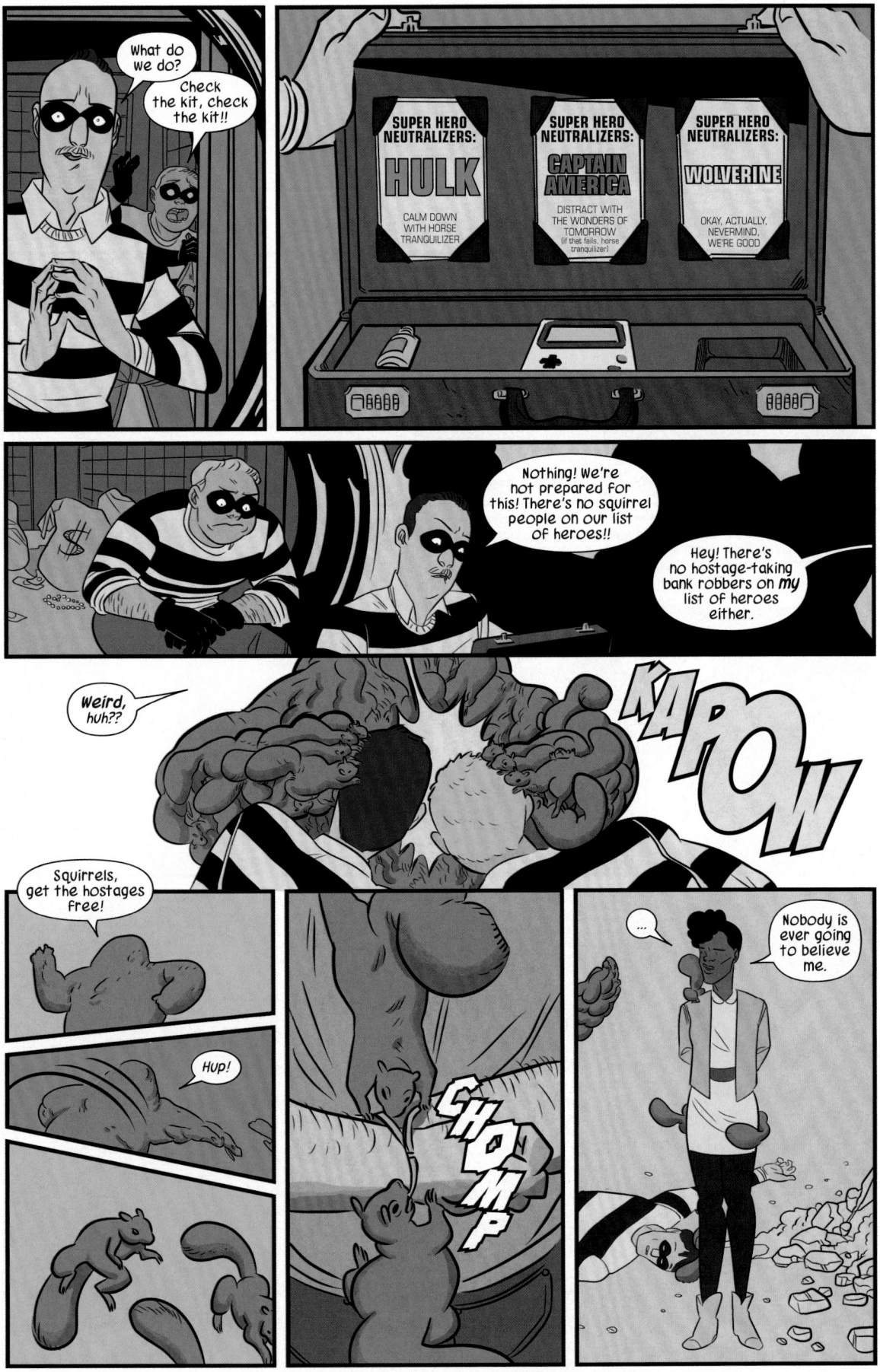

This is worse than the time that famous actor guy stole my fries right out of my hand!

How many other squirrels wear pink bows? Is it a lot? I never really noticed squirrels until now.

It's almost like we're fighting a literal force of nature given squirrel form! But hah hah hah THAT'S CRAZY

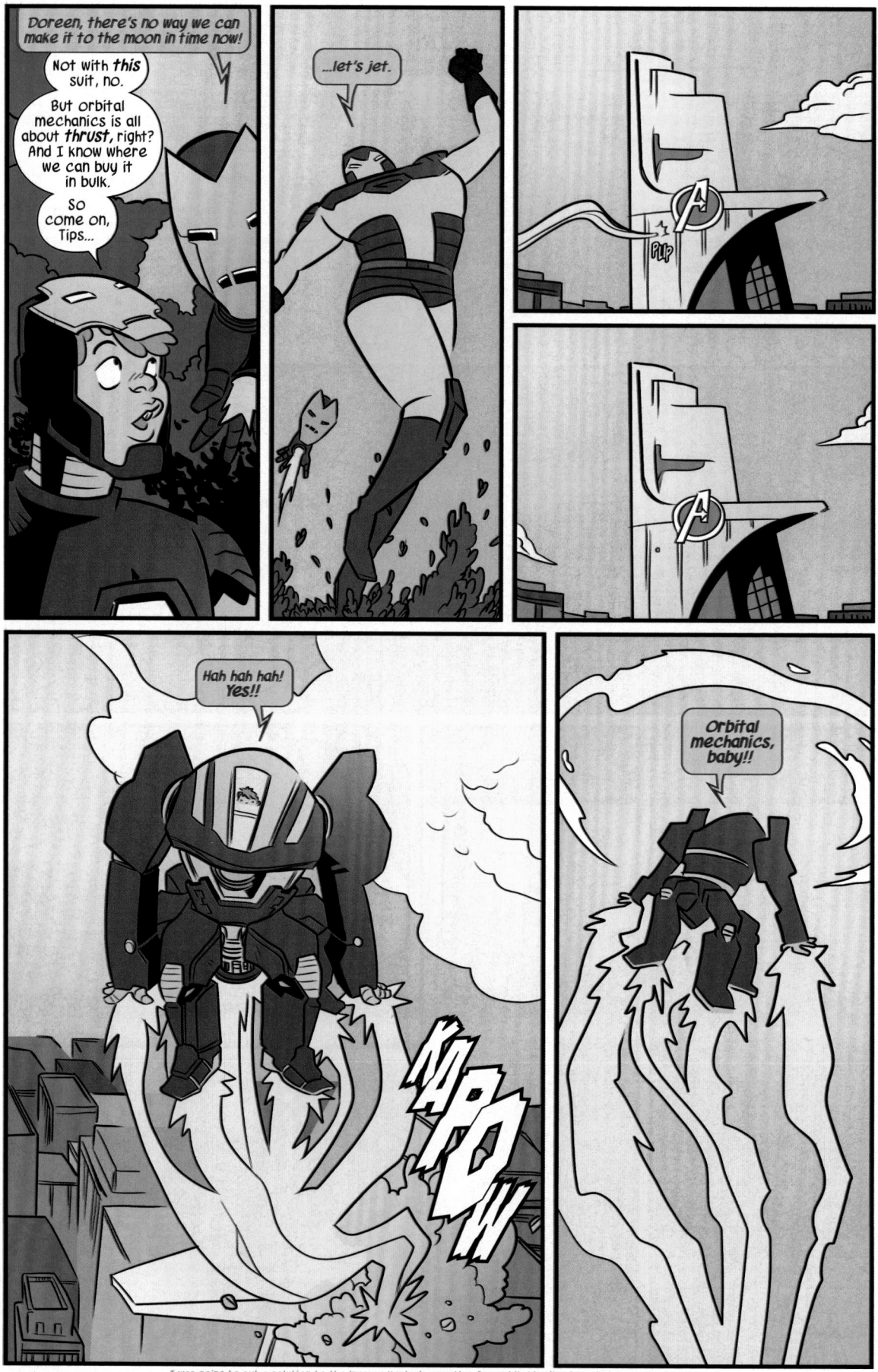

I was going to put a solution to the inverse Kepler's equation for orbital bodies here but ran out of room, so you'll just have to take my word for it that the physics in my talking squirrel comic are 100% ultralegit

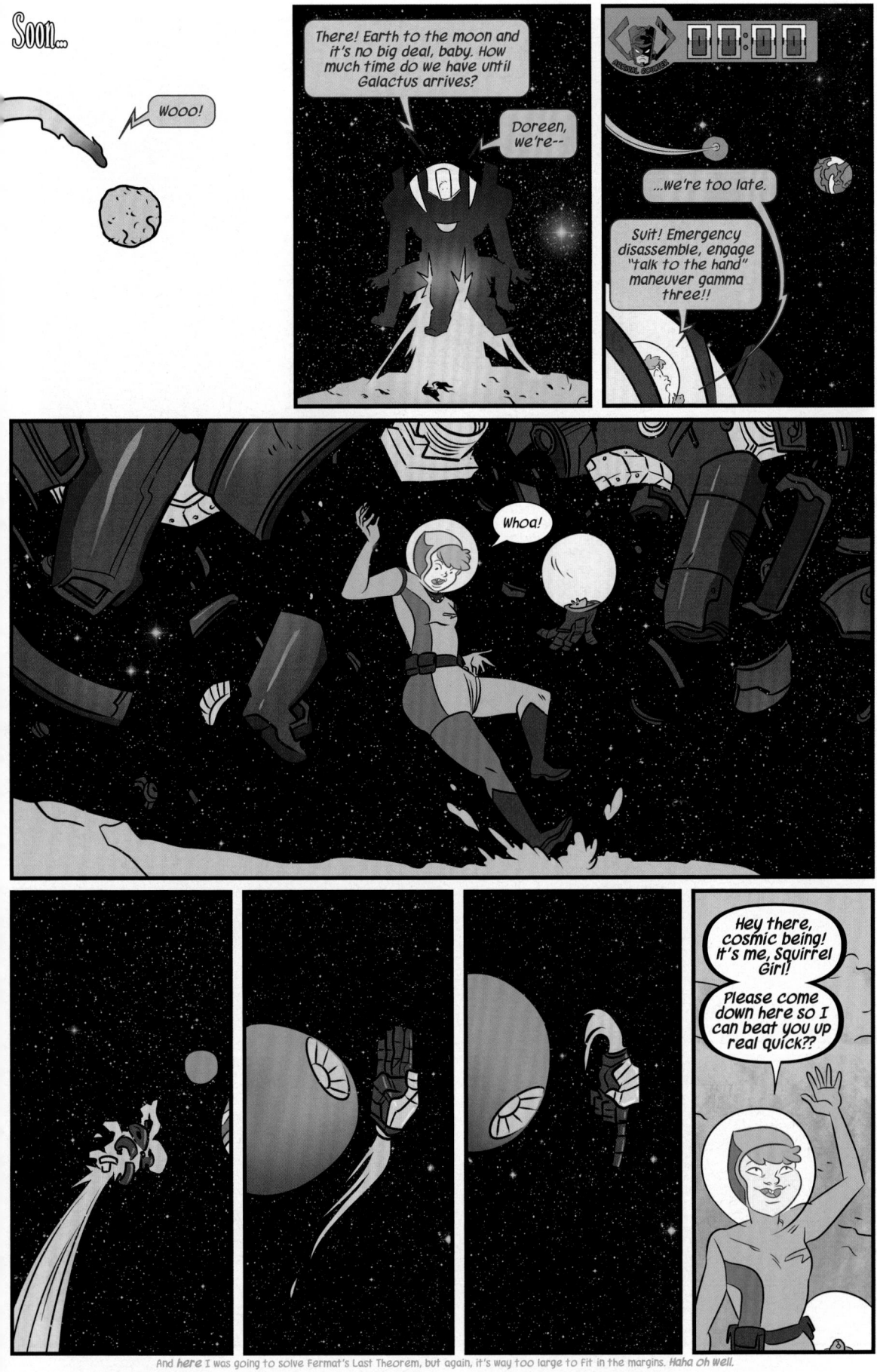

And *here* I was going to solve Fermat's Last Theorem, but again, it's way too large to fit in the margins. *Haha oh well.*

What are you reading down here for? They're about to fight!!

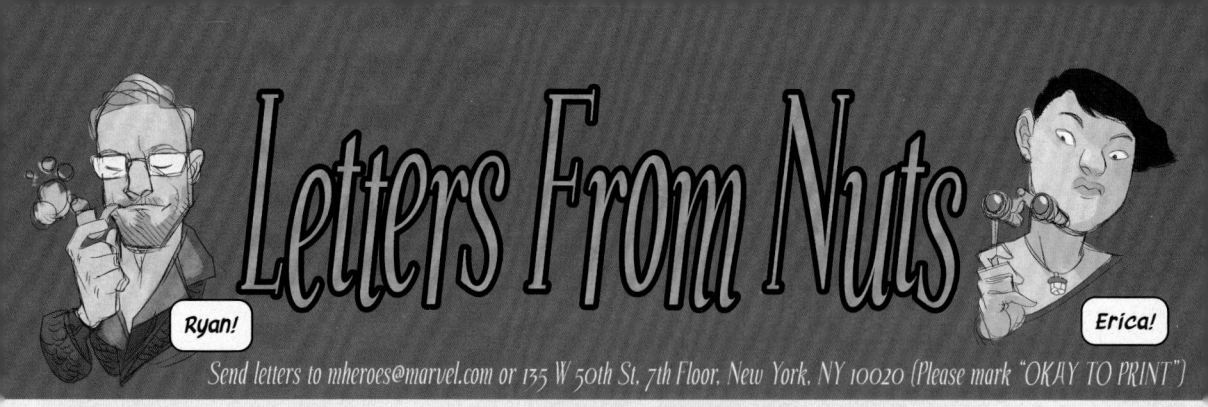

Send letters to mheroes@marvel.com or 135 W 50th St. 7th Floor, New York, NY 10020 (Please mark "OKAY TO PRINT")

Welcome to the special triple-sized you-guys-are-awesome-and-are-really-vocal-about-your-feelings-for-this-book letters page!!!

Q: Do squirrels and kitties usually get along? Are you concerned that Tippy-Toe and Mew will come to blows?

Michelle K.

RYAN: They don't usually, I think! But Tippy-Toe and Mew aren't your usual squirrel and kitten. Besides, Nancy would never have said it was okay for Tippy-Toe to stay with them unless she was already PRETTY SURE Mew was on board.

Dear Ryan, Erica, Rico, & VC's Clayton (or just Clayton, idk),

You guys, your Squirrel Girl comic is the coolest! Ryan, I've followed your writing online for a number of years, and have been SUPER PUMPED to see you busting out of the internet and on to printed paper held together by staples!

Can we expect to see some Asgardian tomfoolery within these pages? I demand a Doreen vs. Thor/Tippy-Toe vs. **[CENSORED]** throwdown/team-up! I mean, come on, Norse mythology has **[MEGA CENSORED]** (whose name, I learned today, means **[YES, THIS TOO IS CENSORED]** which is pretty cool)! How are you NOT going to use that?!

Keep up the amazing work, everybody!

Adam Barnett
Portland, OR

RYAN: Thanks, Adam! We are actually planning to see that person you mentioned showing up down the line, so I just went ahead and censored your letter here as to not spoil the surprise. I'm sorry! But when it happens you can say "See? CALLED IT" and point to this page for proof. Attention future generations: ADAM WAS TOTALLY RIGHT.

ERICA: Hah! That character might have been the topic of my first frantic middle-of-the-night email to Ryan about Squirrel Girl matters. My first foray into self-publishing was a little bestiary and [REDACTED] is totally in there. I love that dude.

Dear Nutty Buddies,

Thanks so much for producing a title that I can confidently share with my niece, Paislee!

We're both nuts for Squirrel Girl and it's refreshing to know there's a strong, positive, female role-model out there in the Marvel Universe for her to admire on a monthly basis as she grows from being just a tiny little acorn herself.

Here's a question for you: Did you know that in Norse mythology there was **[CENSORED FOR THE EXACT SAME REASONS AS THE LAST LETTER]**? Really! **[THIS OTHER BIT IS CENSORED TOO. EVERYONE, YOU ARE TOO GOOD AT GUESSING OUR STORY IDEAS]** - and then **[AGAIN, CENSORED, SORRY, I GUESS??]**.

Nuts over you,
Paislee H. & Darryl E.

RYAN: Paislee is adorable! #1 Paislee fan over here. Also: I'm glad we're putting out a book you can share with her once she's old enough to realize that if she looks at a certain idiosyncratic series of squiggles in the right order she can hear a voice in her head telling her a story! Once that happens we will be ALL OVER that.

Hi Team Squirrel Girl!

My friend and I just finished the first issue and we both loved it! But we are concerned about Squirrel Girl! Will she have time to go to her classes with all of the crime-fighting that she'll be doing? What are her classes? Thanks!

Beck and Bida

RYAN: I haven't seen her full course selection, but I know there's Introduction to Database Systems, Introduction to Compilers, Linear Algebra, Punching Dudes 101, etc. But yeah, it's tough to balance your social life and your studies. That's why I recommend crime-fighting students cultivate arch-enemies whose powers can dovetail nicely into your education. For example, a super villain who along with trying to take over the world also constructs linear equations in n-dimensional Euclidean vector spaces would be ideal, because that way you can LEARN as you TURN him away from his life of crime.

Q: Now that Squirrel Girl is in college, will she join any clubs or sports teams?

Zachariah W.

RYAN: Zachariah, you clearly wrote this letter before issue #2, where we saw her attempts to join some clubs! So since your question has already been answered, I'm gonna pretend you asked a different question. LIKE SO:

Q: Squirrel Girl has the proportional speed and strength of a squirrel, so what would happen if she got shrunk? Would she lose her powers?

Zachariah W.

RYAN: Excellent question, Zachariah!! This question has not been asked before and I'm glad you definitely came up with it on your own just now. The answer is that while her speed and strength are proportional TO her normal size, they don't change WITH her size. If Ant-Man shrunk her, she'd still be super tough. Similarly, if she ate a bunch and got heavier, that wouldn't make her any stronger. It's too bad, because that would be the EASIEST and MOST FUN way to enhance your super powers ever!

Q: What breed of squirrel is Tippy-Toe? There are 256 species of squirrel worldwide so it's pretty hard to narrow it down.

Sarah Yu
Hong Kong

Squirrel Enthusiast

RYAN: Sarah, I'm glad that as a Squirrel Enthusiast there is finally a comic for you! I don't know what species of squirrel Tippy-Toe is, because while I too am a Squirrel Enthusiast, I am a rank amateur. Are there any Professional Squirrel Enthusiasts who can determine Tippy-Toe's exact squirrel type out there?? (No, "rad type" does not count as an answer.)

ERICA: WELL. I think as someone who gets paid to think about and draw squirrels, I can count myself as a Professional Squirrel Enthusiast, Ryan. Tippy-Toe joined the team after the untimely death of Monkey Joe (RIP) while Doreen was a member of the Great Lakes Avengers, who are based out of Milwaukee. Wisconsin has five varieties of tree squirrel: grey, fox, red, northern flying and southern flying. Tippy is clearly a grey squirrel. Fun fact: Grey is a variety and does not necessarily reflect the actual color of individual animals.

Dear Ryan, Erica, and Rico,

THE UNBEATABLE SQUIRREL GIRL #1 has to be one of the best comic books I've ever read. It was funny, cool, quirky, wacky, and a lot of other good things. Thank you for giving us such an awesome comic book with great art and writing. It's nice to have another super-heroine who doesn't go around fighting crime in her underwear. Some people think the art is "too cartoonish" but 'TIS NOT TRUE! THE ART IS PERFECT!

The Mighty M

P.S. Where can I read Nancy's Cat Thor fan fiction? And where can I get that Purl Jam poster?!

RYAN: Thanks! I actually really like how Squirrel Girl dresses in layers, because you gotta figure sometimes it'd get too hot or too cold and you'd want to be able to adjust. It's just sensible!! As for Nancy's fan fiction epic Cat Thor: Cat God of Cat Thunder, I'd love to have that show up at some point, but for now it lives only in our dreams of a better, impossibly perfect world.

ERICA: Ahhhhhh! Thank you so much! I think clothing choices are pretty important in getting across who someone is. Some people do want to run around in their underwear and that's great for them (looking at you, Emma and Namor), but that's not everyone's bag. I don't want to get too deep into it but our clothing choices say a lot about what we want to get across to people, even if you're not actively thinking about what you're putting on at the time. I mean, you still had to go out and buy it, or, if you're a super hero, probably MAKE IT. I want the clothes to feel like something those characters would choose for themselves.

Hey guys!

Keep up the good work with Squirrel Girl. It's refreshing to see a female super hero that has the body type a lot of us girls have. How did you guys come up with the character design?

Can't wait to read more!

Alexa

ERICA: For the body, I didn't think about it much. I tend to draw super heroines with more physical powers thicker because I honestly have a hard time believing that a 90-pound woman can take down a 200-pound steroidal dude who has equal fighting ability. So yeah. Her body type in the book is the same as the first finished drawing of her I

ever did because that's just how I see Squirrel Girl. Besides, have you seen people who do crossfit? Their thighs are HUUUUUGE.

Hey gang,

I rarely if ever write in to comics but I had to drop a line regarding SQUIRREL GIRL #1 to let you guys know I think it's great stuff. I've been a fan of SG since the GREAT LAKES AVENGERS specials back in the day and it's nice to see the character step out into her own series. My hope was that this would be a return to fun comics without the gloom and grit teeth so prevalent in most titles on the stands and I am happy to report you guys hit it out of the park with a funny, entertaining read. Kudos!

Galactus in the second issue? Nice. I guess Franklin Richards is going to need a new herald after SG gets through with him, huh? I think a college dorm lacks the space for a trophy room to keep the giant purple moon boots, so a headquarters might soon be an item on Doreen's To-Do List. . .

Thanks again for a great comic!

Take care,
Stacy Dooks

This book is so much fun. I had no earthly intention of buying it, I liked the character, and I really enjoyed the Dan Slott GREAT LAKES AVENGERS miniseries from a decade ago, but Squirrel Girl as a lead? My budget is paper thin, and I didn't even consider it. But then the reviews came pouring in, all overwhelmingly positive. And I thought about how disillusioned I've become as a comics fan. Neverending event series, tie-in series to the events, ret-cons, deaths that last six months to spike sales, major changes to flagship characters that everyone knows won't last, another fun She-Hulk series getting cancelled, FANTASTIC FOUR getting shelved, I'm sick to death of it. I thought "this might be what I need." Something purely fun, unapologetically upbeat.

So I bought it, and I laughed out loud at nearly every page. It was so funny. This is exactly what I needed right now. A comic to remind me why I love comics. And now Squirrel Girl is going to fight Galactus. This is going to be incredible. You could do an issue where she does nothing but converse with Tippy-Toe while onlookers look on in bewilderment, and I would love it. Between this and ANT-MAN #1, this has been the most enjoyable week I've had reading comics in at least a decade, I'm completely serious. I truly hope the fanboys and fangirls sample this book, because if they do, it will last.

Jason Smith
Buena Park, Ca

RYAN: Jason this is the nicest! You sure know how to make a guy feel good about his squirrel lady comic: thank you. Our secret is we're just making the sort of book we'd like to read, and we've been really lucky that other people want to read it too. Hooray for comics!

ERICA: I think it's been said before, but I think we were all worried/curious about the reception of this book. It's definitely different from what people associate with mainstream comics so I'm glad that you like it and that we can fill that gap for you.

Dear Ryan North, Eric Henderson, and the Squirrel Girl gang,

I always loved Squirrel Girl and was sad to see how it wasn't appearing as a solo issue in recent years. As a result, when I heard that Squirrel Girl was getting its own series I was jumping up and down like a squirrel would seeing an acorn!!! The art also brings out the best of the college story of Squirrel Girl. It is awesome seeing how Squirrel Girl isn't depicted as a dark, gritty super hero, but a cheerful, just super hero and the art brings out the best of that. I really am honored to be reading this issue and I wish this story continues on forever!!! The jokes make me laugh a lot and her cheerful attitude makes me blissful too!

Thanks,
Andre Lee

P.S. I totally love squirrels in real life too!

RYAN: Thanks Andre! Funny thing about squirrels in real life: I never noticed them before, and now I see them EVERYWHERE. So I'll be walking my dog Chompsky to the park and see squirrels in the trees and think "Oh right I'm late on the issue #5 script, I should get on that." So now there's these reminders for me to get back to work distributed WORLDWIDE, on every continent except Antarctica.

Therefore I'm moving to Antarctica, see y'all later!!

Dear Ryan & Erica,

When in 1933 a bunch of newspaper comic strips were put together in a periodical, thus creating the first comic book, if its creators could only know that it would one day lead to THE UNBEATABLE SQUIRREL GIRL, they would have reveled with paroxysms of joy, knowing with happy certainty that they had played such a crucial role to the betterment of Western Civilization.

I could go on, but I fear I might start to tilt toward a touch of hyperbole.

Gene Popa

RYAN: One of my favorite things to think about is how your entire life has technically been leading up to THIS one moment, right now. So if I've just made a good sandwich, my entire life has been leading up to that one delicious sandwich. Then a few seconds later my life has been leading up to me eating it, then cleaning up the dishes, etc. Anyway, Gene: my ENTIRE LIFE has been leading up to me answering your letter just now. Thank you for sending it in!

To the nut that answers these letters,

I have been waiting years (make that 2) for Squirrel Girl to have her own comic book series and when I finally got my hands on issue #1, I went absolutely nuts! And if THE AMAZING SPIDER-MAN can have a 700 issue run, then surely, THE UNBEATABLE SQUIRREL GIRL can have at least 800...I mean, 001 on the cover does mean there's room for up to 999 issues, right? Which brings me to a totally unrelatable question...I know Squirrel Girl speaks English as well as Squirrel and is going to school to learn to speak 1s and 0s, but does she speak any other languages such as Japanese, Chinese, Spanish, or Chipmunk?

Philip Hanan

RYAN: Hah hah, I did not notice until JUST NOW that our book does have two leading zeros on the cover. It's not issue 1, it's issue 001. So that's 999 comics in total that Marvel expects from us, and at one a month, that's...83 ¼ years?! LET THIS BE A LESSON TO US ALL: always read the contracts BEFORE you sign them, lest you find out in a letters page you have SIGNED THE REST OF YOUR LIFE AWAY.

Still. No regrets!!

ERICA: Did you know that chipmunks are also part of the family *Sciuridae?* They are! They probably speak the same language. PROBABLY.

Q: Will Squirrel Girl ever team up with any female characters to kick some major butt?

Maryam F.

RYAN: Yep! AND HOW.
ERICA: ALL THE BUTTS.

Dear Erica and Ryan and Rico,

I just finished the first issue of THE UNBEATABLE SQUIRREL GIRL and I am vexed. I was wondering: How can I be more like Squirrel Girl? I am neither a girl nor a squirrel and have a severe nut allergy. The doctors say I shouldn't even be alive! What should I do?

Your Scholar,
James Kislingbury

RYAN: Okay first off, if you're going to doctors who say "you shouldn't even be alive," you should get a new doctor. Get one who says "you SHOULD be alive and I'm glad you are, holla" instead. And while you might not be able to be Squirrel Girl, you could still be Chipmunk Hunk!

ERICA: Well, the important thing with squirrels isn't so much nuts as much as they're opportunistic omnivores that can't digest cellulose. So try to find foods that have a lot of protein, carbs and fat.

To the inspired minds behind THE UNBEATABLE SQUIRREL GIRL,

I'm gonna be honest here - Squirrel Girl wasn't a hard sell for me. I like comics, I like squirrels. I'm a girl and I like reading about girls. In the title alone Squirrel Girl has almost everything I like in life (still needs: Oreos, posters, high speed car chases, etc).

So I figured I was going to like SQUIRREL GIRL #1 because HOW CAN YOU NOT and then I read it (as I made my own move to college, funnily enough) and was STILL wowed! I AM IN LOVE! It is so much fun, from start to finish! The dialogue is hilarious, the facial expressions are to die for, and the colors are so vibrant and delightful ajskdlfjkasdfj IT IS SO. GOOD.

I can't wait to see more of Doreen's adventures - crime-fighting! Attending classes! Punching and studying, aw yeah! It's all great. Fingers crossed for a long and happy series for Doreen and co.!

Marley

RYAN: Thanks, Marley! You're RIGHT that we haven't had high-speed car chases yet, but it's been tricky because how often do you see squirrels inside a car? INFREQUENTLY AT BEST. I guess... we could change that?

Guys and Gals,

You're all nuts. Irrevocably and gloriously so. ANT-MAN? SQUIRREL GIRL? Astonishing and unbeatable first issues!

More importantly, my sick four-year-old was so engaged as we read (an edited, age-appropriate version of) these comics out loud to her (along with issues of ROCKET RACCOON and MS. MARVEL, whom she loves); it lends such a positive experience to her being in a hospital. In times past (the early 80s), I actually looked forward to plowing through back issues of EARTH'S MIGHTIEST while recuperating from surgery or high fever. Isn't that nuts?

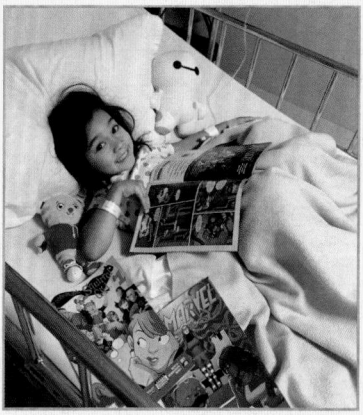

That's probably because every True Believer knows that Marvel Comics are the best medicine.

Nuts, but true.

Papa Joe
Cville, VA

P.S. I do hope Kamala Khan and Doreen Green make it to the MCU!

RYAN: Joe, this is adorable and I wish I got comics when I was sick. I hope your daughter is feeling better and never makes the causal connection between illness and GETTING TO READ ALL THE COMICS EVER, because if I had as a kid I'm sure I'd be faking tummy aches every week.

Dear Erica, Ryan, and Rico,

I've just finished reading issue #1 of your new series and I have to say I absolutely loved it. The humor is spot on, the art is ADORABLE, and she has the best theme song ever.

Also, I've been wondering where I can get myself a pack of those Deadpool super villain trading cards? I could really use them in my top secret crime-fighting endeavors. (Maybe I shouldn't be mentioning this in a, possibly, published letter.)

Sarah Y.
Hong Kong

RYAN: Sarah Y. from Hong Kong, your secret of fighting crime is safe with me! I won't tell anyone that Sarah Y. in Hong Kong fights crime. Also, I would love to see those Deadpool cards in real life

too, but I'm a little worried because then they'd need me to write descriptions for EVERY SINGLE MARVEL VILLAIN EVER IN TIME, which I dunno, might take a while. A long weekend, easy.

First off, thank you so much for giving Squirrel Girl her own comic, it's a breath of fresh air and something I have been waiting for...forever. Because squirrels. Second, yay! The bestest and most awesomest marvel heroine gets some recognition for saving us all from the real threats! Yay again!

Um...this was just a thank you letter really, but if I had to ask questions. Ok. Love the addition of acorn earrings, but have the eye stripes gone for good? They were cute...

Also, any chance we get to meet the parents? Doreen's mum and dad must be the proudest parents, or the most laid back, ever.

I have another thank you, to Ryan and Erica, thank you for giving us an upbeat and completely positive lighthearted book, in an industry where everyone is dark, edgy and gritty. (And depressing... Is it me? Or has every hero got problems? Except Squirrel Girl who has squirrels!)

Love you all!
Tim P.
Plymouth, England.

ERICA: Can you imagine having to take that makeup on and off every time though? Squirrel Girl's back in NYC and there's NO TIME TO STOP FOR ANYTHING.

Dear Squirrel Girl Team,

Hello there, you fabulous people in comic book world! When I heard that they were going to be bringing Squirrel Girl back to the Marvel Universe, I was all filled with glee and dancing a jig. I let that simmer on the back burner, until I heard that Ryan North would be writing it. I can't actually put into print how excited this made me. I guess to go with my previous metaphor, you could say I boiled over. (This is the part where you all are laughing and telling me how clever I am; at least, it is in my head.) I've seen what you can do with six panels of dinosaurs, and I am among those who helped with that Kickstarter of yours for the *Hamlet Choose Your Own Adventure.* Who better to take the helm of this new series?

From the second I pulled the first issue off of the shelf at my comic store, I knew I would not be disappointed. The art is amazing! Doreen didn't look quite how I pictured the new Squirrel Girl to look, but that's okay because she looks even better. I love that pretty much everything is round and colorful. Makes the book so much more approachable to someone like me who is new to the world of comic book buying/collecting. I wish I had a convention coming up so I could cosplay her already. And the story! I want to ask so many questions about where you are heading, but I think I'm just going to wait until the comics come out. Thank you all for your work that you're doing. I look forward to seeing what adventures lay ahead for Doreen and Tippy-Toe. And on that note, I'm off to see if Rosetta Stone offers a course on the Northeastern variant of Squirrelese.

Your Unbeatable Fan,
Stefanie M.

RYAN: Thank you, Stefanie! And I am secretly really excited for convention season this year, because I really want to see the Squirrel Girl cosplay. Everyone dress up as her forever, thanks in advance!!

UNBEATABLE SQUIRREL GIRL was the absolute highlight of my day, week, and possible even year (though it's a little early to tell). I'm so excited to see Doreen not only put bad guys in their place but also tackle the exciting world of Computer Science - how incredibly rad. It's the kind of book that gives me hope for super-hero comics. In the mean time, I have two questions for you:

1) Will any of Doreen's past friends (the GLA, Devil, or the Cage-Jones family) be making appearances?

2) If Doreen could have lunch with any other Marvel super hero who would it be?

Congratulations and I'm sure you'll continue to knock it out of the park.

Arielle B.

RYAN: I know Erica loves Flatman (AND WHO DOESN'T?) so I'd love to have him appear at some point! Of course, who's to say that he hasn't ALREADY appeared, only he was standing at just the right angle as to be invisible? WHO INDEED. Well in fact it's the artists and writers who can say, and we're here saying he hasn't done that in Squirrel Girl.

YET.

ERICA: If Doreen could have lunch with any other hero it would be Dazzler because, oh my god, she has, like, ALL of her albums.

Dear Squirrel Girl Creative Team (can I call you the Squirrel Squad?)

I'm absolutely nuts about Doreen! Thank you for bringing back one of my favorite Marvel characters from obscurity into a book I can shove in all my friends' faces. The first issue was all I hoped it would be and more.

I am foaming at the mouth for the next one already! (I should probably go get that checked out.) I am curious, how did you choose between Tippy-Toe and Monkey Joe to appear in the series?

Amy Chase

Ok I've been obsessed with Squirrel Girl and waiting for this moment for a while now... great job on the first issue! I really wanted her to kick some major butt in the first issue but next one looks pretty crazy so I already can't wait.

I MUST know what her MJ necklace stands for. If it's Marc Jacobs I will die but I think there's another meaning... Also, I need her purse, any idea where I can get one?!

Last, Squirrel Girl needs to go into psychiatry or psychology. She has a way with talking to this guy that shows a gift.

Love,
Squirrel Girl super fan for life

RYAN: It stands for "Monkey Joe," her first squirrel companion! He was the squirrel she hung out with before Tippy-Toe. It could also stand for "My Jewelry," in case she only wears jewelry that describes itself. They only way to confirm that for sure though is if she ever wears earrings that just say "earring," which I think... might be amazing??

ERICA: I totally own a brown version of that purse. I think it's sold out. I'm sorry. I'm just going to be honest here, I pretty much own all of Doreen's clothes.

I want to say "chitter chit chit chitter" THANK YOU for bring Squirrel Girl back. The fact that she wears the MJ in homage to Monkey Joe makes me want to tear up.

I can't wait for the next issue! My squirrel friend Ladro is throwing nuts at me asking how he can join the squirrel army?

Sincerely,
Beth 'the Squirrel' Jankowski

ERICA: I'm glad I'm not the only one who tears up over Monkey Joe. (RIP)

Hi Squirrel Girl Team!

So I'm writing this on a Tuesday night because I run a shop and I totally stayed late tonight just to read your book.

I just want to say going in I wasn't convinced. I wasn't a fan of the art, but by the second page (that we hadn't seen in the preview yet) I was totally won over. I love it! I can't wait to sell this to everyone that comes in tomorrow and days after that until I run out then I can sell the 2nd and 3rd and 4th printings too, and the hardcovers and trade paperbacks. This book rocks and it will be great for anyone that loves fun and maybe we can win over some of the people that hate fun too.

One little thing, any chance the color on the bottom page tidbits can be altered a teensy bit? They were really hard to read. Or I just need new glasses.

Thanks for the fun comic!

Jenn Swackhamer
Comic City Pontiac, MI

Hello!

First off, I have to say how absolutely MARVELlous (ha!) the first issue of UNBEATABLE SQUIRREL GIRL was! Wow! Artwork and writing combined, it's pretty much the most perfect comic book of all time and space.

Secondly, I have to say how super AWESOME it is to have another female-fronted book, but also one where the character is hilarious and clumsy and endearing and basically a lot more like me than any of the other beautiful, graceful super-women out there. (I love them too though!) I love everything you've done and I absolutely canNUT wait for the next issue! (One day I'll stop with the puns. Today is NUT that day.)

Holly Ringsell

Well, we've used up all the extra room we have this month! But keep writing! We want to hear from every dang one of you! And don't forget to check out our behind-the-scenes tumblr: unbeatablesquirrelgirl.tumblr.com! See y'all next month! Stay nutty!

Next: Squirrel Girl vs. Planet-Eating Man!

ISSUE #1 VARIANT COVER BY **SIYA OUM**

the unbeatable Squirrel Girl
VS

Doreen Green isn't just a first-year computer science student: she secretly also has all the powers of both squirrel and girl! She uses her amazing abilities to fight crime **and** be as awesome as possible. You know her as...**The Unbeatable Squirrel Girl!** Let's catch up with what she's been up to until now, with...

Squirrel Girl *in a nutshell*

GALACTUS @xGALACTUSx
HEY GUESS WHAT I'M COMING TO EARTH TO DEVOUR THE ENTIRE PLANET

GALACTUS @xGALACTUSx
AND NOBODY KNOWS BECAUSE I PUT MY SHIP IN A STEALTH FIELD

GALACTUS @xGALACTUSx
"BUT WAIT," YOU SAY, "AHA! NOW WE KNOW YOU'RE COMING BECAUSE YOU JUST POSTED IT ON SOCIAL MEDIA!!"

GALACTUS @xGALACTUSx
ONLY YOU AREN'T SAYING THAT BECAUSE NOBODY KNOWS I'M COMING BECAUSE NOBODY FOLLOWS ME ON THIS STUPID SITE

GALACTUS @xGALACTUSx
...

GALACTUS @xGALACTUSx
#ff @xGALACTUSx

Tony Stark @starkmantony
@unbeatablesg Just heard more of my Iron Man parts have been "borrowed," and now there's a big hole in my building too. Any ideas?

Squirrel Girl! @unbeatablesg
@starkmantony Oh wow dude these suits have wifi in them??? I can go online on my way to the MOON?? Tony ur the best <3

Tony Stark @starkmantony
@unbeatablesg That "wifi" works even in Mars orbit, uses proprietary Stark technology, and costs several thousand dollars a kilobyte.

Squirrel Girl! @unbeatablesg
@starkmantony um I already downloaded some songs for the trip to the moon. Sorry!!!

Tony Stark @starkmantony
@unbeatablesg Don't reply to say you're sorry! That ALSO costs money!

Squirrel Girl! @unbeatablesg
@starkmantony sorry sorry!

Tony Stark @starkmantony
@unbeatablesg Don't reply! Stop replying!

Squirrel Girl! @unbeatablesg
@starkmantony whoooooooooooooooooooooooooooops

Nancy W. @sewwiththeflow
Story time, friends. Your hero, me, thought she'd eat some delicious (cash-only) falafel. So I went to the bank.

Nancy W. @sewwiththeflow
And you know how banks are always the worst even when you're NOT being taken hostage? WELL GUESS WHAT?

Nancy W. @sewwiththeflow
Yep. But then we got saved by @unbeatablesg who appeared in SQUIRREL SUIT ARMOR MODE. Not even joking.

Nancy W. @sewwiththeflow
This really happened. I was saved by a squirrel suit Squirrel Girl. I know you don't believe me.

Nancy W. @sewwiththeflow
tl;dr: doesn't matter, ate falafel

Whiplash @realwhiplash22
I am trapped in #CentralPark and need #squirrelrepellant, PLEASE RT!!!!! #please #rt #please #rt #please #rt

search!

- #bankrobbery
- #banksnobbery
- #mew
- #squirrelsuitcrochetpattern
- #snackcakes
- #squirrelman

All right! Now to the letters page, and then the rest of this book is just blank pages! Haha, *Oh well!!*

Dear Squirrel Girl comics,

I really liked Tippy-Toe's squirrel armor. I can't believe that Squirrel Girl's fighting Galactus. I mean, that's a big thing, you know! I find that the cover is very funny because Squirrel Girl is using Iron Man as a surfboard. I mean, a surfboard? That's cray-cray!

Signed,
Elsa McQuaid

RYAN: Thanks! To invent Tippy-Toe's armor I held out my hand in an approximately squirrel shape and confirmed, yes, that would fit inside a glove. And if you're reading this, then you just read the page that showed the aftermath of Squirrel Girl beating Galactus off panel, which we can all agree was really very satisfying! Writing: it's easy!!

ERICA: I remember getting an e-mail saying we needed the second cover and that it should be Squirrel Girl surfing on an Iron Man suit and my first thought was "That's stupid." I'll admit when I'm wrong-- just don't tell Ryan I told you that. Any part of that.

Dear "Letters from Nuts" crew,

As a comic collector of over 20 years, I want to thank you for creating such a great comic. Over the past several years, my love of comics has crossed over with another love - squirrels! I have been a squirrel fanatic since my college days when I worked on an independent study project to identify squirrel parasites. In the last few years, I have been taking a sketchbook to the comic conventions that I attend and I have been asking various artists to draw a Squirrel mashed-up with any character of their choosing! I have attached several of the sketches for your enjoyment (including some of my own):

Question: Based on Marvel's summer plans, is there any way we could get a small landmass on Battleworld assigned to a whole universe where all of the Marvel characters are squirrels (and maybe Squirrel Girl could rule them all)? In my opinion, that would be the most important part of the Secret Wars crossover!

Your loyal fan,
Corey Fuhrer

RYAN: Those pictures are amazing. If only we had made this comic more than one page long, we could've shown you Squirrel Galactus! But alas, we decided to publish this book with only one page of comics, some letters, and then a whole bunch of blank pages.

I have pitched your idea to Marvel and they informed me that it's "way too late" to rewrite their Battleworld plans to include Squirrel Island, although they "wish they had thought of that sooner" and "feel regret about not doing Squirrel Island more keenly than [they] have ever felt any emotion before, including love." So – that's something!

ERICA: Although we SHOULD do Squirrel Island but like Spider Island. (Because let's follow up on ALL of Dan Slott's ideas.) Everyone on Manhattan gets bitten by radioactive squirrels but nobody turns into a Squirrel Girl equivalent because that's not how she got her powers. Pretty sure this is a one-page story. Is NOT BRAND ECHH still a thing?

Is Chipmunk Hunk perhaps a monk? Look, I'm just trying to think of rhymes for the theme song.

Stephen,
Kansas City

RYAN: All I know for sure is: he's been shrunk, he can dunk, spelunk, his car's got a trunk, and if you bring him to a cabin he'll steal the top bunk.

ERICA: RYAN. Leave the rhyming to the professionals. Like Adam WarRock. Have you HEARD his Squirrel Girl rap? (www.adamwarrock.com) Step down, buddy.

My four-year-old twin daughters enjoy squirrels quite a bit. They are always asking if we can leave some peanut butter and crackers outside to feed our neighborhood squirrel crew. They also love comic books, as they've been exposed to them pretty much since they were born. So, it was a no-brainer to hip them to THE UNBEATABLE SQUIRREL GIRL series.

There aren't very many comics that the girls will allow me to read them from start to finish. They generally prefer to tear through 'em on their lonesome, looking at the artwork and making up their own dialogue. SQUIRREL GIRL is one of the exceptions though.

One constant with each issue I've noticed is that they keep asking me where Gamora is. So if you end up having the Guardians of the Galaxy make an appearance, that would seal the deal with their appreciation of Squirrel Girl.

Darrick Patrick
Dayton, Ohio

P.S. I'm including a photograph of Nola and Logann showing off their Unbeatable collection so far:

RYAN: Awesome, a complete set! You can tell Nola and Logann that I, the writer of these comics, say that Gamora is secretly there, just hidden. She and Doreen were going to get lunch together before Doreen got wrapped up in this Galactus thing, so while Doreen's there fighting Whiplash and bank robbers and Galactus, Gamora's standing there, just out of frame, gesturing

to her watch, impatiently waiting.

ERICA: Yes! My favorite compliment this book gets is being able to share it with your kids, so I love that! Side note: peanuts aren't great for squirrels and apparently can get some sort of weird invisible toxic mold (citation needed)??? If you want to leave a snack out, nuts in shells are great. It's something they love and the shell provides good gnawing exercise.

Well Hi there!

This is why I really like Squirrel Girl: she's really funny-looking. On a new-comics wall, I can look across all Marvel's titles; lots of angry-looking, grim but very buff-looking hero-suited figures, and there's Squirrel Girl, happy and goofy-looking. I have to support that. And apparently she's the most powerful super-powered person in the whole Marvel Universe? Y'know, I get a lot of comics, but now I'm down to just two Marvel comics, this one, and Captain Marvel. Guess I just like strong, pleasant women in my life. Carol and Doreen are like that, nice people. One's goofy-looking: y'know? -- in the Marvel Universe, that just makes her exceptional.

It certainly helps that SQUIRREL GIRL's written well. And works well with a slightly 'cartoony' edge to the artwork. The words and pictures really support one-another. You could do me a favor, though, by using a darker ink to your teeny tiny bottom-page typings. Old eyes, y'know? Thanks for a good, fun comic.

Best wishes,
Matt Levin
Hatfield, MA

ERICA: I'm glad you're into it! I really stressed out when I was first asked to draw this character. One of the only pieces of mine that Wil (our editor) mentioned when we were starting out was a much more realistic-looking movie poster I drew, and I went back and forth on how the style should look. In the end I took a gamble on a looser and more animated look and I'm super happy that it's worked out.

Loved, loved, loved UNBEATABLE SQUIRREL GIRL #2. Art and story - killing it! Thank you for this book.

Any chance we'll see the Great Lakes Avengers at some point? I mean, that's where I first met Doreen, and now she's way more popular than the GLA so it'd be nice to use her popularity to bolster them up. Also, when you inevitably get to your big, triple-sized anniversary spectacular, could you reprint her first appearance? It's not an easy "tail" to come by. Thanks!

Charles Albert,
Richmond VA

RYAN: I'd like to! I really like Flatman because he has all the powers of being a man AND all the powers of being flat. I can't tell you how many times I've looked at tiny cracks under doors and wanted to see what was on the other side and said "If only I was a flat, but alas, I am a man." Okay, I can: it's several. I have done that several times.

ERICA: I keep picturing the GLA reunion like a high school reunion and Doreen is the one kid that left their small town to do something big and is home for the first time in 10 years and just has no idea if it's going to be super awkward or not. Also, everyone is worried Deadpool is going to show up. THAT GUY, AMIRIGHT?

I just wanted to thank you guys for starting to write/print this comic at such an opportune time. Just two weeks ago I was mentioning that Squirrel Girl existed to a friend and he didn't really believe me, so I looked her up to show him and simultaneously found out that these were being printed! Now, hopefully, I'll get to show him a physical copy with my name in it! It also gives me a great read to look forward to every week with my best-friend-roommates. So...Thank you for such a humorously written and expertly drawn comic!

On an unrelated note though, any chance of us ever seeing any physical copies of Deadpool's Guide to Super Villains and Super Villain Accessories in the future?

Andre W.

RYAN: I'd love to see the Deadpool cards as a set! I don't know if anyone higher up at Marvel Headquarters reads the letters page of our squirrel comic BUT IF THEY DO: Yo, that's two months in a row people have asked for these cards! Please make them immediately. PS: this counts as market research, and I have never been wrong before.

ERICA: Henderson and North, MAKING IT HAPPEN. (The comic/continuation of Squirrel Girl, not the cards. We don't really have control over merchandising- yet.)

To whom it may concern,

I got the first two issues of UNBEATABLE SQUIRREL GIRL recently, and I can't wait to for next month's issue. Thank you for making Tippy-Toe so cute, and for Nancy. I knit and crochet, too (and now I know next year's Halloween costume). I couldn't resist making a little Tippy-Toe for myself. Thank you for creating something so cute and fun.

Keep up the amazing work!
Katie H.

RYAN: Katie, GUESS WHAT: I love that Tippy-Toe so much! Nancy's knitting is inspired by my mom, who made me a sweater with a dinosaur on it, and the sweater has a hood with a tassel, AND THE DINOSAUR ON THE SWEATER IS WEARING THE SAME SWEATER WITH THE SAME HOOD AND TASSEL. It's the best ever.

ERICA: AHHHHH. WHAAAAAT. I do some sewing, but knitting and crocheting are amazing mystery arts to me. I'm so in awe! That Tippy is just so cute! Fun Fact: When I first saw Nancy in the script she was so much like a friend of mine that I grew up with that I had to reread her intro a few times. When issue 1 came out, other friends asked if it was her. So I love that people are getting into Nancy because she rocks!

Hey guys,

Thanks for making such an epic comic, first of all! Secondly, I really like Mew and also knitting. How can I join Mew Club?

Jane
Cat, Squirrel, and Yarn Enthusiast

RYAN: To join Mew Club you have to write down "Mew is a great cat" on a piece of paper and sign your name, and then you are a member of Mew Club. Mew is based on two cats we know in real life (one I know, and one Erica knows) and when you perform this ritual, we will be alerted, and will inform the Actual Mews of this Actual News.

Wanted to say that, as one of two comics I'm reading, this one is my personal favorite. Just wanted to ask, have you ever come across negative reception for the comic? How did you deal with it?

Felix

RYAN: Thanks for reading our comic! Also, you should read more comics!

There's always going to be people who don't like what you're doing, and it's like, that's fine? There are books I don't like but I don't hate them or want them destroyed or anything. I just don't read them! So if I see someone reacting negatively to anything I do, I don't take it personally, I just think "Oh that's too bad, this person's tastes are not my own. I guess their opinions are different from my clearly objectively correct ones, oh well."

ERICA: I'm with Ryan. There are going to be some people that you just don't agree with on taste and even if they're jerks about it there's not much you can do there, so there's no point in dealing with that. The only time I address it is when I get "won't read because Squirrel Girl isn't hot anymore" because UGH. Anyway, it's pretty easy to get those dudes to back off with a quick "why are you so concerned about a minor being hot?" Also, I'm so curious about this one other comic you're reading. Tweet us about it when you see this answer!

Next: Readers Beware!

Yep, that hidden message at the bottom of that earlier page was a lie! Downside: *I'm an unreliable secret message narrator.*
Upside: Hey, at least this comic isn't a total ripoff now, right??

SCIENCE CORNER: You're in space right now, too! You're on a ball of *liquid metal* surrounded by rocks and a thin layer of gas, spinning wildly through the universe at thousands of kilometers per hour. Hang on tight!

If the Power Cosmic is anything like an acorn, *and I'm pretty sure it is,* then we should bury it in the ground and then forget where we buried it and then a Power Cosmic tree will grow from that spot many years from now!

Yes, Galactus can talk to squirrels. He can also fire lasers out of his eyes, and *obviously* by the time you unlock "Level 1: Laser Eyes" you've already mastered "Level 100: Chatting Up Tiny Mammals"!

EVERYONE WAS ALL "OH LOOK IT'S GALACTUS, I THINK HE'S GREAT BUT THE ONLY WAY I CAN EXPRESS THIS ADMIRATION IS TO STYMIE HIS PLANS, NEVERTHELESS I DO SECRETLY REALLY RESPECT WHAT HE'S TRYING TO DO HERE"

IF YOU SEE HIM, TELL HIM I SAID HE'S SO UNCOOL THAT HE'S NOT JUST A SQUARE...HE'S A COSMIC CUBE

Turns out you ***can't*** defeat Galactus by just chilling with him on the moon! All right, Tippy, scratch that OFF the list, and we'll see how well *"Fight him in orbit* ***around*** *the moon"* works out.

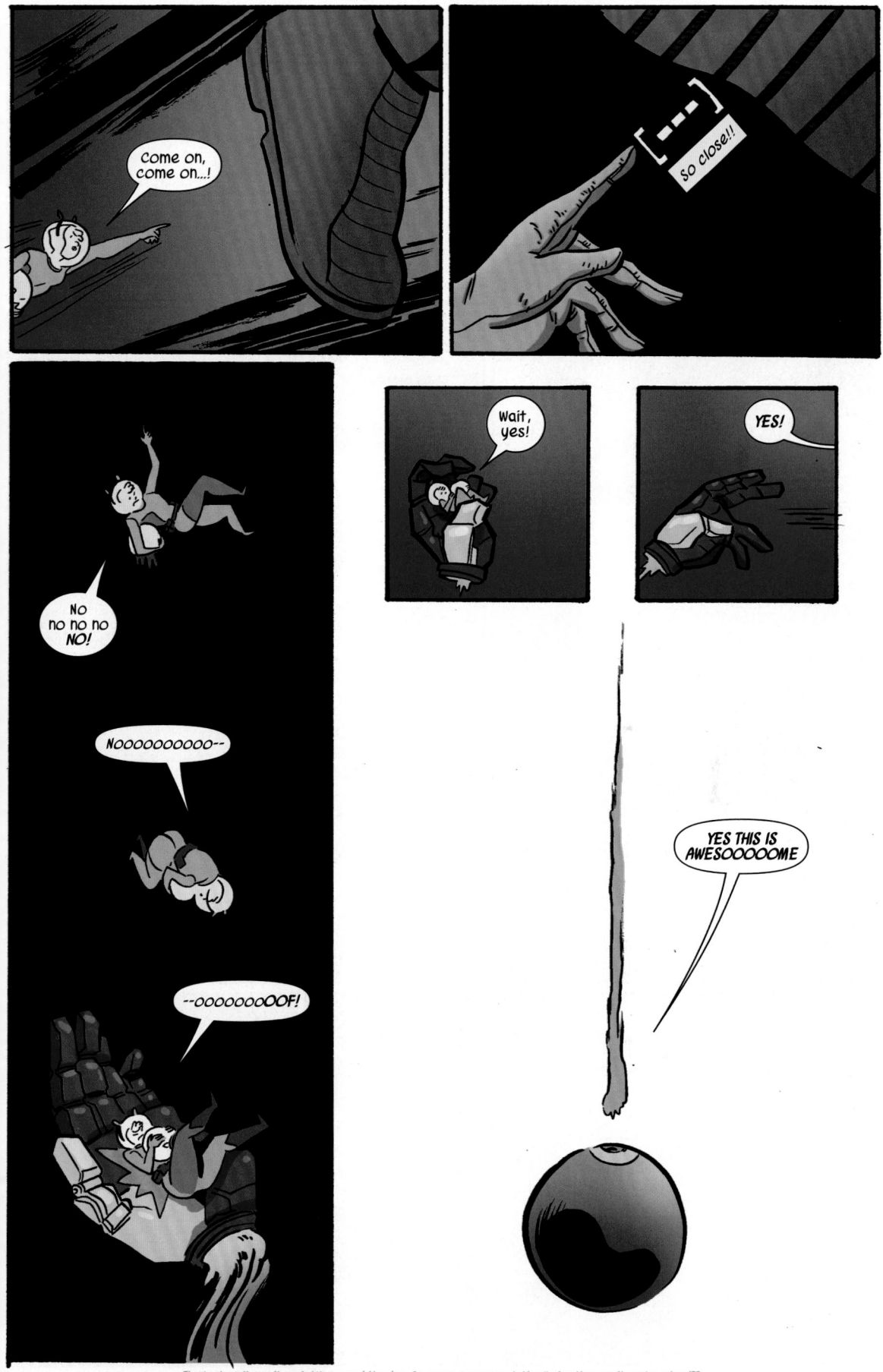

Thanks, Iron Man suit parts! You saved the day. Come on, everyone, let's all give those suit parts...a hand??

Alternate password suggestions: GALACTUSRULES, G@L@CTUSRUL3Z, I<3CONSUMINGALLLIFEENERGY

And you definitely don't defeat Galactus by having a more audacious fashion sense. Many have tried, all have failed, though honestly many of them looked pretty great while they did so.

Galactus, I don't know what your computers actually look like, but that retro computer interface had ultra-primitive terrible security.
Do I thank you, or thank my imagination, or...?

SWOOOF
SWOOOF
On second thought, Galactus, maybe you **should** eat Earth instead of this planet??
Tippy!!
DUDE, I'M SORRY, BUT THIS PLACE IS THE GREATEST!

So in conclusion, then we came back to the moon to lie down because we all over-ate, and here we are!
NO REGRETS
Oh, dude, you're awake! Can you send me back to Earth now?
I got class tonight and I'm kiiiinda super late. I could take the Iron Squirrel/Iron Giant-Hand-Thingy but I'm pretty sure I've used up all its fuel by now.
SURE NOT A PROBLEM
BUT BEFORE YOU GO I WANTED TO GIVE YOU A LITTLE SOMETHING
AND YOU SHOULD KNOW THAT AMONG THE MANY POWERS OF HE--
--OR SHE--
--WHO WIELDS THE POWER COSMIC IS THE ABILITY TO READ MINDS
SO I ALREADY KNOW YOU'LL LIKE IT
No way.
NO way.
Oh. Oh, Galactus.
I love it.
DEADPOOL'S GUIDE TO SUPER VILLAINS
CARD 1 OF 4622
GALACTUS
- DEVOURER OF WORLDS
- WIELDER OF THE POWER COSMIC
- ...AND A FRIEND
CALL ME IF YOU EVER WANT TO GET INTO HERALDING

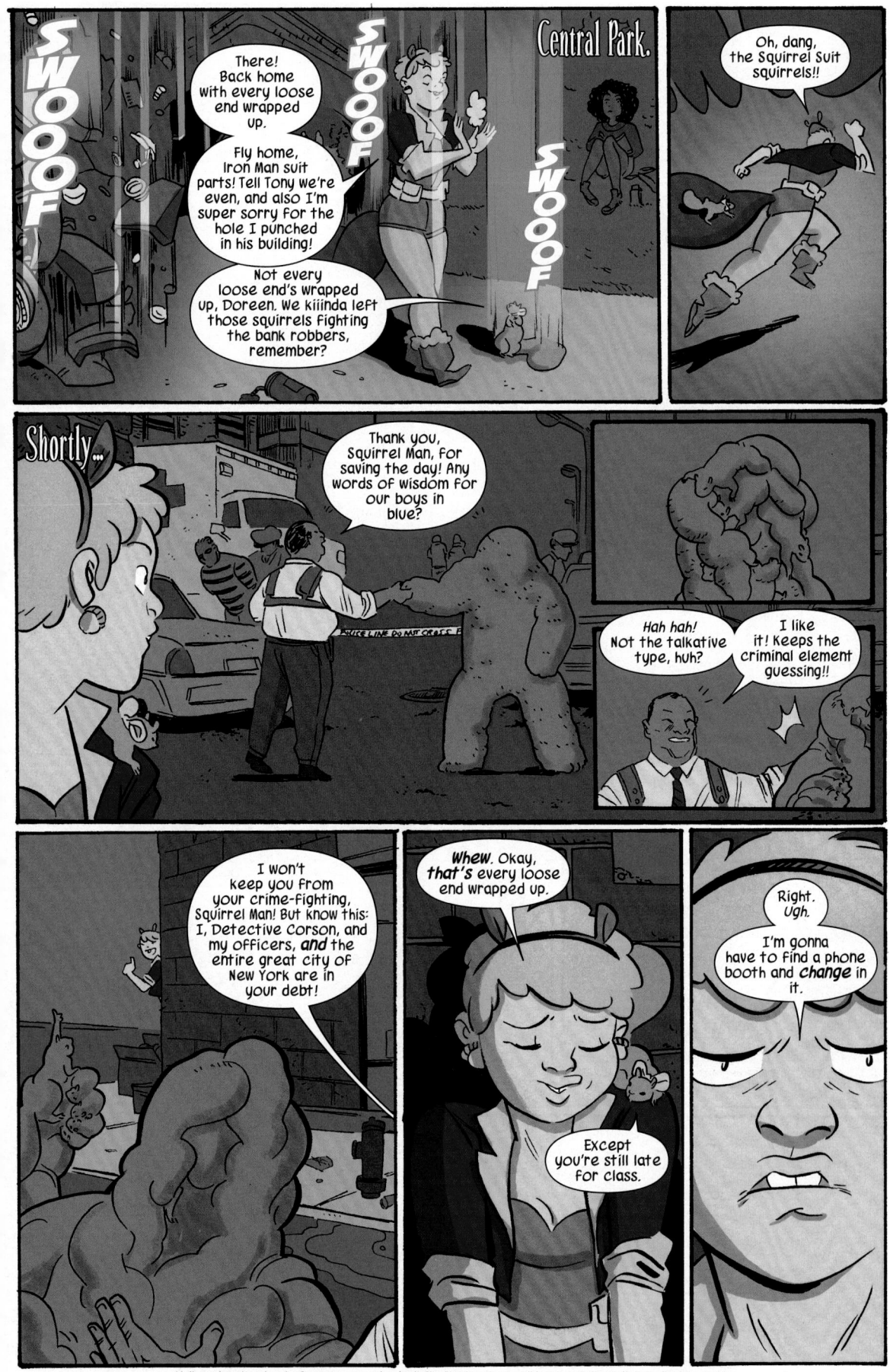

Well, you're almost out of power, so maybe don't fly. Slowly walk or roll home, Iron Man suits!! You're free now!

Oh, don't worry, that's not you! That's my new 100% original character named "Squirrely D. Girly." TRADEMARK AND COPYRIGHT BY ME, DO NOT STEAL!!

Doreen, do you even know where Ireland is? Doreen, do you need to take Intro to Really Basic Geography before you take Intro to Compilers??

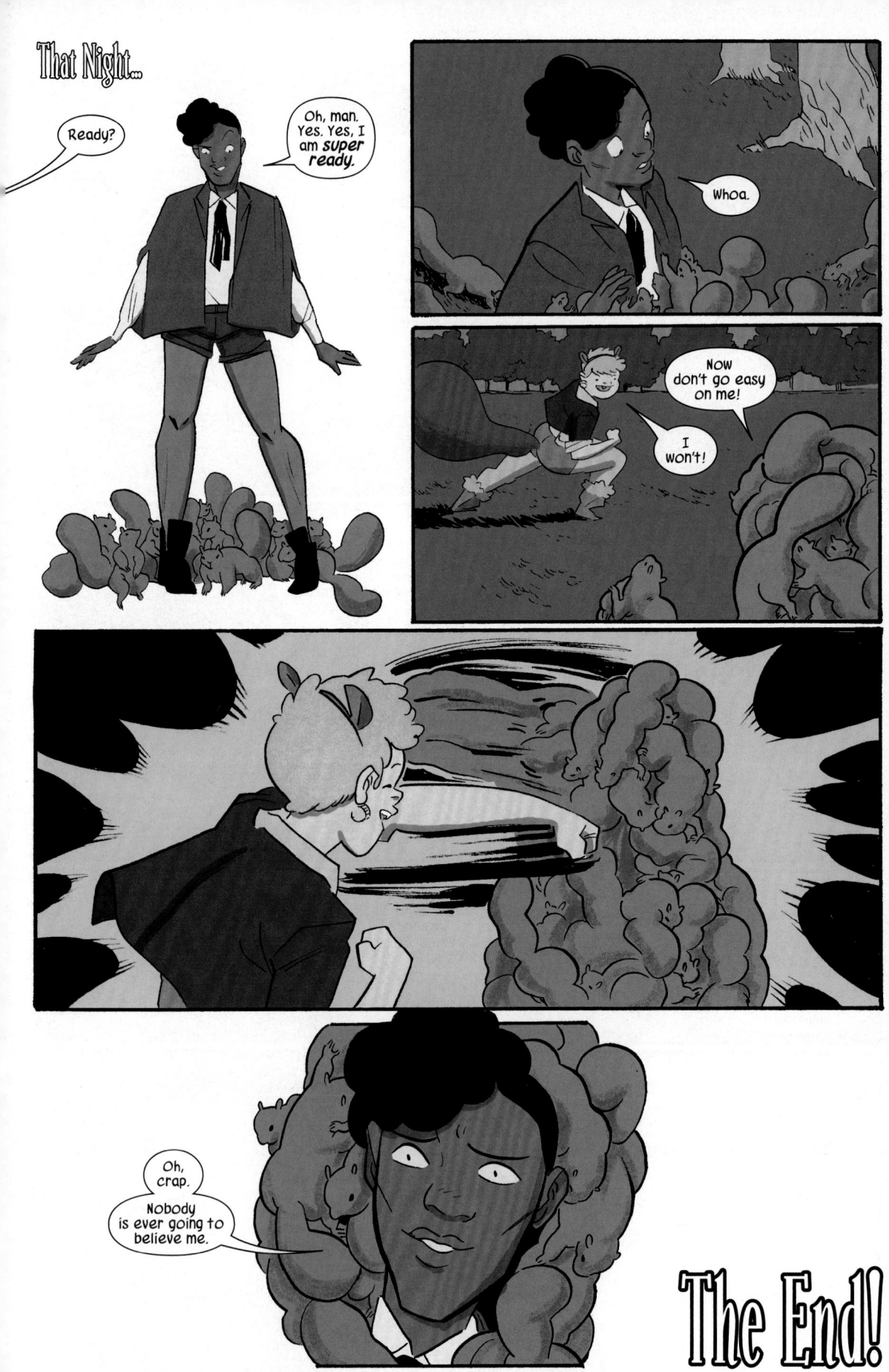

Tomorrow's headline: MYSTERIOUS SQUIRREL MAN SPOTTED WITH CAT?? CAT IS NAMED MEW AND SEEMS KINDA SURLY BUT STILL MEGA CUTE.

Written by
Ryan North

Art by
Erica Henderson

Trading Card Art by
Chris Giarrusso

Color Art by
Rico Renzi

Lettering and Production by
VC's Clayton Cowles

Cover Artist	Erica Henderson
Special Thanks to	Cassie Hart Kelly
Assistant Editor	Jon Moisan
Editor	Wil Moss
Executive Editor	Tom Brevoort
Editor in Chief	Axel Alonso
Chief Creative Officer	Joe Quesada
Publisher	Dan Buckley
Executive Producer	Alan Fine

Squirrel Girl will return in...
Squirrel Girl #5, duh.

I swear, animals, you can let me go now. I promise I won't whip **any** of you.
We understand each other, yes?
Hey, you like nuts, I will get you nuts. So many nuts. I will knock over a bulk food store and give you eighty-five percent of the take, yes?? No, no, **ninety-five** percent.
Animals?
Animals, I really really have to go to the bathroom.

MARVEL SUPER-HEROES #8

STAN LEE PRESENTS:

the coming of... SQUIRREL GIRL!

STEVE DITKO - PLOT, PENCILS, INKS
WILL MURRAY - SCRIPT
CHRISTIE SCHEELE - COLORS
BRAD K. JOYCE - LETTERER

TONY STARK IS SWEATING NOW.
PING!

WITH GOOD REASON.
PING!

PING!
HE CAN'T SEE A THING...EXCEPT INTERNAL DIGITAL READOUTS.

AND HE'S ZIG-ZAGGING THROUGH A CHOKED STAND OF TREES NEAR STARK ENTERPRISES AT OVER 90 MILES AN HOUR!
PING!
NOW I KNOW HOW THE EARLY ASTRONAUTS FELT--BLASTING THROUGH SPACE STRAPPED INTO A WINDOWLESS CAPSULE.

BOOT JETS LIFTING ME UP...
MUST BE A HORIZONTAL BARRIER DIRECTLY AHEAD.
PING!
PING!

OKAY, TONY. I GUESS YOU'VE GOT A BACK-UP IN THE ALWAYS-POSSIBLE EVENT YOU'RE BLINDED OR BLACK OUT IN FLIGHT.
PROVIDED YOU SURVIVE THE TEST RUN.
UNBEKNOWNST TO THE ARMORED AVENGER, A TWITCHING-TAILED FIGURE CROUCHES ON A TREE-BRANCH, WAITING TO POUNCE.

WHICH IT DOES WITH UNERRING SKILL.
WHA...?! EITHER I'VE BEEN ATTACKED...

...OR THE CAR SYSTEM HAS JUST DEVELOPED A MAJOR BUG.
WHOEVER YOU ARE, YOU'VE MADE A BIG MISTAKE.
JUST BECAUSE I'M WEARING THIS ALLOY BLINDER DOESN'T MEAN I CAN'T DEAL WITH YOU!

CAN'T SHAKE HIM.
AND HIS PROXIMITY IS CONFUSING THE CAR SYSTEM.

ALL RIGHT, LET'S SEE EXACTLY WHO YOU ARE!

NOT YET! NOT YET!
SOMETHING WHIPPED INTO MY EYES. FEELS LIKE...
FUR?

BEEP
BEEP BEEP
UH-OH! CAR OVERLOAD WARNING SENSOR JUST KICKED IN!

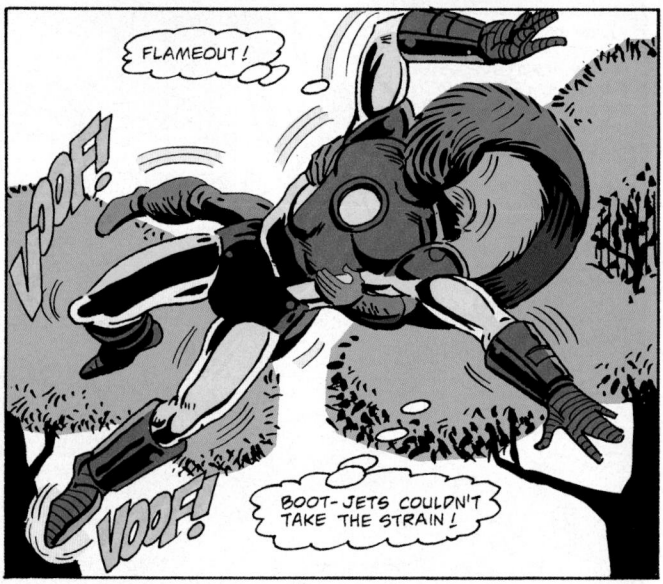
FLAMEOUT!
VOOF!
VOOF!
BOOT-JETS COULDN'T TAKE THE STRAIN!

ONE COLD COMFORT.
HE'S GOING DOWN WITH ME.

WHAT ON EARTH?

HI! I'M SQUIRREL GIRL.
SQUIRREL GIRL?

YEAH. NEAT NAME, HUH?

WELL, IT DOES RHYME.
WHAT'S THE IDEA OF JUMPING ME?

I JUST WANTED TO SHOW YOU HOW ROUGH AND TOUGH I CAN REALLY BE.
ROUGH AND TOUGH?

I FIGURED I'D HAVE TO PROVE MYSELF BEFORE YOU'D TAKE ME ON AS YOUR FIGHTING PARD.
PARD?

WHAT MAKES YOU THINK I WANT OR NEED A PARTNER?
EVERY HERO SHOULD HAVE A PARTNER. DON'T YOU KNOW THAT?

BESIDES, I LIKE YOU. YOU'RE MY FAVORITE AVENGER.

ALSO, I LIVE AROUND HERE, WHICH MEANS I CAN BE HOME IN TIME FOR DINNER.
UNLESS WE HAVE ANY REALLY BIG ADVENTURES IN CHINA OR MEXICO OR CONNECTICUT--NEAT FARAWAY PLACES LIKE THAT.

I SEE, HOW OLD ARE YOU?
FIFTEEN--WELL, FIFTEEN NEXT JULY, ACTUALLY.
BUT WHO CARES ABOUT DUMB STUFF LIKE THAT?

DON'T YOU WANT TO SEE MY POWERS?
POWERS?

SURE. I HAVE PLENTY OF POWERS. I'M A MUTANT.
BUT DON'T TELL ANYONE, OKAY? IT'S KINDA EMBARRASSING.
MY LIPS ARE SEALED.
WHO WOULD BELIEVE ME?

WATCH THIS!

I CAN DO ANYTHING A REAL SQUIRREL CAN DO...

JUMP. CLIMB. HOP.
PLUS, I'M EXTRA, EXTRA NIMBLE.
AMAZING...

TA-DAH!
OKAY, YOU CAN HOP. SO CAN THE HULK.
WHAT ELSE?
WATCH. NOTHING UP MY SLEEVE.
PRESTO!
CHK!
IT'S MY KNUCKLE SPIKE.
IRON MAN + SQUIRREL GIRL
I HAVE FINGER CLAWS, TOO, BUT THEY'RE TOO LITTLE FOR FIGHTING. GREAT FOR CLIMBING, THOUGH.
NOT EXACTLY IN WOLVERINE'S CLASS, ARE YOU?
YOU COULDN'T SHAKE ME OFF YOUR BACK SO EASY, COULD YOU?
GOOD POINT.
IS THAT ALL?
PLAYING HARD TO GET, HUH?
CHECK IT OUT. I CAN CHEW THROUGH SOLID WOOD WITH THIS BABY. GROSS, HUH?
IS THAT... TAIL REAL?
MY MOM THINKS IT'S THE CUTEST THING. BUT SHE DOESN'T HAVE TO HIDE IT IN HER JEANS.
SO WHAT'S THE VERDICT, AVENGER?
I CAN CALL YOU THAT, CAN'T I?
SQUIRRELS... THEY'RE RODENTS, AREN'T THEY?
WELL, YEAH. SORT OF. BUT THEY'RE NOT RATS OR ANYTHING.
WE'RE MUCH PRETTIER.
WE?
I CAN TELL YOU'RE NOT IMPRESSED.
OH! I FORGOT TO MENTION--I CAN TALK LIKE A SQUIRREL, TOO!

LISTEN.
CHITTY CHIK CHUK!
UH, VERY NICE. REALLY. YOU CAN STOP NOW.
CUK CUK CUK
DIDN'T I SOUND JUST LIKE A SQUIRREL?
YOU'VE CONVINCED ME. BUT I WOULDN'T EXACTLY CALL THAT A POWER.
ACTUALLY, THERE'S MORE TO IT THAN THAT...
WONDERFUL. MY WOULD-BE PARTNER, WHO TALKS LIKE A SQUIRREL.
CUK CUK CUK CUK CUK CUK CUK
WHAT?
ABOUT TIME YOU GUYS SHOWED UP.
THESE ARE YOURS?
THEY UNDERSTAND EVERYTHING I SAY!
CUK CHRT
CUK CUK CUK
HOW DO YOU GET THEM OFF?
EASY. YOU JUST GO 'CHUTTY CHET CHET!'
OF COURSE.
CHITTY
CUK CHRRT?

YOU KNOW, I'LL BET THE X-MEN WOULD BE VERY, VERY INTERESTED IN TALKING TO YOU.
NO WAY!
SPAWK
GUK

I DON'T WANT ANYBODY TO KNOW I'M A MUTANT.
BESIDES, THEY'RE ALL SO STUCK UP--ESPECIALLY THAT OBNOXIOUS KITTY PRIDE.

I KNOW--WHY DON'T I INTRODUCE YOU TO CAPTAIN AMERICA & HE'S USUALLY OPEN TO NEW PARTNERS.
GUK
GUK
DOWN, MONKEY JOE!

I DON'T BELIEVE THIS. YOU'RE REJECTING ME!
IT'S NOTHING PERSONAL. HONESTLY.

I REALLY DON'T NEED A PARTNER. IRON MAN IS A SOLO ACT.
BUT...BUT YOU'RE MY PERSONAL HERO! YOU CAN'T SAY NO!

AND YOU'RE UNDER AGE.
SORRY. I CAN'T BE RESPONSIBLE SHOULD SOMETHING HAPPEN TO YOU.
SNIFF!

NOW IF YOU'LL EXCUSE ME, I'M RUNNING LATE.

WAIT! THERE'S ONE OTHER THING.

I DON'T KNOW HOW TO TELL YOU THIS, BUT ON MY WAY TO STARK ENTERPRISES, I-I KINDA SORTA HAD MY FIRST SUPERFIGHT.
CONGRATULATION CONGRATULATIONS.
WITH WHO?
I THINK.
WE WERE NEVER PROPERLY INTRODUCED, BUT HE WAS ONE OF THOSE ARMORED GUYS.
THE CRIMSON DYNAMO?
DON'T THINK SO. HE WAS GREEN.
NOT TITANIUM MAN? HE WEARS GREEN ARMOR. OR DID.
NO, THIS GUY'S ARMOR WAS GRAY. IT WAS HIS CLOTHES THAT WERE GREEN.
GRAY ARMOR... GREEN CLOTHES.
NOT--
PRECISELY, AVENGER.
DOCTOR DOOM.
UGH!
HOLD STILL, PLEASE.
CRRNN
OH NO! YOU HURT HIM!
HIS ELECTRONICS HAVE MERELY EXPERIENCED A PULSE-INDUCED INTERRUPTION.
AS FOR YOU, FOOLISH GIRL...
SSSSSSSSSS

DO YOU NOT UNDERSTAND THAT NO ONE MAY ATTACK THE ROYAL PERSONAGE OF VICTOR VON DOOM WITH IMPUNITY?
LOOK, IF I HAD KNOWN THAT WAS YOU, I WOULD NEVER HAVE JUMPED YOU LIKE THAT.
I WAS ONLY TRYING TO IMPRESS IRON MAN SO HE'D BE MY PARTNER. YOU KNOW?

INSTEAD, YOU SHALL HENCEFORTH BE KNOWN AS THE UNWITTING INSTRUMENT OF HIS DOWNFALL.
BOOM

FOR I HAD NO QUARREL WITH IRON MAN THIS DAY, HAVING BEEN ENROUTE TO A RENDEZVOUS WHICH NEED NOT CONCERN YOU.
YIKES! WHAT'S THAT THING?

BEHOLD, THE DOOMSHIP. AN INFILTRATION CRAFT SO LIGHTWEIGHT, SO DELICATELY BALANCED, IF NEED BE IT CAN CROSS A CONTINENT ON THE POWER OF A COMMON CAR BATTERY.
HUUUMMMMMMMM
IT'S HUMONGOUS!

STRUGGLE NOT. FOR THE ANTI-GRAVITY LIFTER IS IRRESISTIBLE.
EVEN NOW, IT IS READING OUR AGGREGATE WEIGHT, MAKING FINE AJUSTMENTS FOR THE BURDEN YOU REPRESENT. I USE THE TERM ADVISEDLY.
GULP! ANY CHANCE YOU'LL TAKE AN APOLOGY?

NONE.
SILENTLY, THE VENTRAL DOORS SLIDE CLOSED.

AND THE DOOMSHIP GHOSTS THROUGH THE TREETOPS LIKE AN ALUMINUM WRAITH.

SOON...
OH, MY HEAD, WHERE AM I?

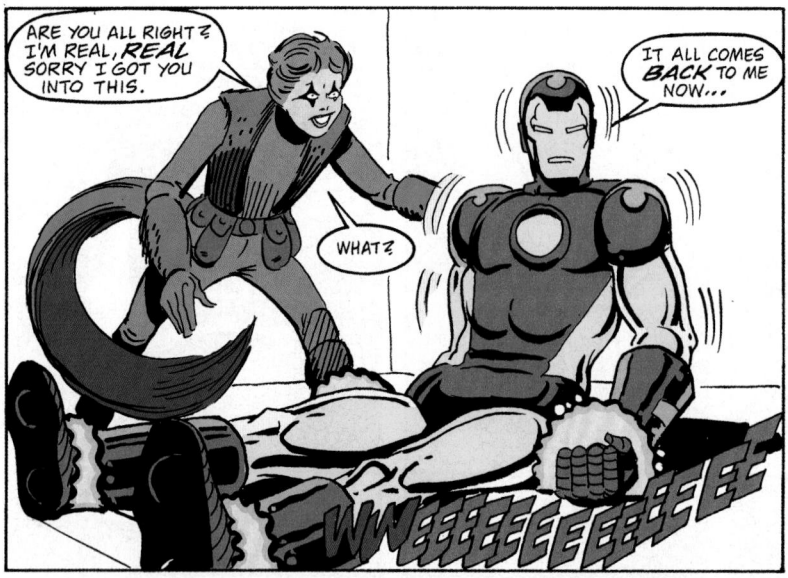
ARE YOU ALL RIGHT? I'M REAL, REAL SORRY I GOT YOU INTO THIS.
IT ALL COMES BACK TO ME NOW...
WHAT?
WWEEEEEEEEEEEE

NEVER MIND.
SOME KIND OF MANACLE... SURROUNDED BY AN ENERGY FIELD.
WEEEEEEEE

STAND BACK. I'M GOING TO... UGH... SHATTER THESE... BONDS.
PIECES MAY... UUHHH... FLY.
RRRSE-AAAARRRRRRR

NO GO. THE HARDER I TRY, THE BRIGHTER THEY GLOW. SOME KIND OF ENERGY SINK, ACCORDING TO MY ONBOARD POWER INDICATORS.
THEY'RE DRAINING... MY ARMOR. CAN'T... BREAK THEM.

BUT YOU CAN'T FAIL! YOU'RE MY HERO!
THERE'S ALWAYS A FIRST TIME.
DO YOU HAVE ANY TOOLS IN THOSE POUCHES?

NO. THIS IS MY NUT STASH. I EAT THEM FOR ENERGY.
TRY SOME MACADAMIAS. THEY'RE GREAT FOR EXTRA PEP.

SOMEHOW, I DON'T THINK THEY'LL REPOWER MY ARMOR.
I ALSO HAVE PEANUTS, CASHEWS, ALMONDS, AND ACORNS.
THOSE I FEED TO MY CRITTERS.
NEVER MIND. ARE WE MOVING?

BRILLIANT OBSERVATION, AVENGER. WE ARE MOVING.
WE ARE ALSO NEARING THE ATLANTIC OCEAN, WHERE I INTEND TO DISPOSE OF YOUR BODIES.
BUT WE'RE NOT DEAD.

THANK YOU FOR REMINDING ME.
KLICK!

RRUM-RRUM
YII! WHERE'D THEY COME FROM?
IT'S NOT WHERE THEY CAME FROM THAT WORRIES ME. IT'S WHERE THEY'RE GOING.

RRUM-RRUM
AND THOSE WELLS IN THE OPPOSITE WALL ARE A MAJOR CLUE.

IRONIC, IS IT NOT, IRON MAN? YOU ARE ABOUT TO DIE BECAUSE THIS SLIP OF A FREAK EMBROILED YOU IN A QUARREL THAT WAS NOT YOURS.

VON DOOM, I DON'T SUPPOSE YOU'D CONSIDER LETTING HER GO?

ARE YOU MAD? TO WITNESS YOUR DESTRUCTION IS FITTING PUNISHMENT FOR HER MEDDLING IN MY AFFAIRS.
IGNORANCE OF THE NAME OF VICTOR VON DOOM ALONE IS SUFFICIENT INJURY TO MY VANITY TO SEAL HER FATE.
BIG TALK, VIC. BUT I GOTTA WARN YOU. I HAVE FRIENDS.

AH, YES. YOUR PRECIOUS SQUIRRELS. I AM SURE THEY WILL GET OVER YOUR LOSS SOON ENOUGH.
SQUIRRELS ARE EMOTIONALLY RESILIENT.

AND NOW, FAREWELL TO YOU BOTH.
RUDE DUDE, HUH?
AT LEAST WE'LL GO QUICK.

RRUM-RRUM RRUM
IT WOULD BE QUICK IF THE SPIKES WERE POINTED. DOOM BLUNTED THEM, SO WE'LL BE CRUSHED TO DEATH SLOWLY.

UKK. DID I SAY I WAS SORRY?
SKIP THE APOLOGIES.
RRUM-RRUM-RRUM

IT'S UP TO YOU. I CAN'T BUDGE WITH MY SUIT DRAINED.
ME?

WHAT CAN I DO? I'M ONLY A...MISERABLE LITTLE RODENT.
JUST LIKE THE KIDS AT SCHOOL SAY.

RRUM-RRUM
TRY.
RRUN RRU
OKAY, OKAY. MAYBE THERE'S A SECRET WAY OUT OR SOMETHING.
LIKE IN A NANCY DREW.

I FOUND SOMETHING! BOY, THIS SUPERHEROING IS EASY.

DARN. IT'S ONLY A VENT.
WE'RE NOT VERY HIGH UP. I SEE TREES UNDER US.

RRUM
DOOM PROBABLY DOESN'T WANT TO SHOW UP ON RADAR.
THE SNEAK.
RRUM RUM

MAYBE I CAN CALL FOR HELP.
CLIK CLIK CLIK

OR AT LEAST SAY GOODBYE TO MY SQUIRREL FRIENDS...
CHIT CHIT CHIT CHEET

ODD. THE STARBOARD PROXIMITY SCANNER IS FLASHING.
PIP PIP PIP

APPROACHING AIRCRAFT? AT THIS PALTRY ALTITUDE IMPOSSIBLE?

NOW THE PORT SCANNER HAS ACTIVATED, AS WELL.
AND VENTRAL.
PIP PIP
PIP PIP

WHATEVER PHENOMENON IS CAUSING THIS, IT RAPIDLY SURROUNDS MY DOOMSHIP.
THE VIEWER SHOULD REVEAL THE THREAT'S TRUE NATURE.

ARE THOSE... SQUIRRELS?
PIP PIP
PIP PIP PIP

THOSE CONFOUNDED RODENTS LEAPING ONTO OVER THE DOOM-SHIP.
PIP PIP

AND I AM UNABLE TO RECALIBRATE THE HYPER-SENSITIVE GRAVITY REPELLERS RAPIDLY ENOUGH TO COMPENSATE FOR THEIR CONSTANTLY SHIFTING WEIGHT.

NO MATTER. ONCE I AM OVER WATER, I WILL DROWN THE INFERNAL CREATURES.
POP
PIP PIP

CHUT?

FORGET YOUR PETS. CALL FOR HELP. HUMAN HELP.
THEY HAVE TO KNOW! WHO'S GOING TO FEED THEM IF I DIE!
WAIT! I SEE SOMETHING!
RRUM-RUM-RRUM

MONKEY JOE!
CHRTT? CHRRT!

YOU CAN STOP STRUGGLING NOW. EVERYTHING'S GOING TO BE OKAY.
ARE YOU SERIOUS? WE'RE SECONDS AWAY FROM BEING CRUSHED TO DEATH.
RRUM RRUM RRUM

MONKEY JOE SAYS EVERYTHING WILL BE ALL RIGHT SOON.
IF YOU DON'T MIND, I'D JUST AS SOON GO DOWN FIGHTING.
OKAY. BUT SQUIRRELS DON'T LIE.
CHUT CHUT

I'LL TRY TO REMEMBER THAT.
HMMM. THERE GO THE LIGHTS.
TOLD YOU SO.

TRY TO BREAK FREE NOW.
MIGHT AS WELL... THESE MANACLES ARE DIMMING.

WHATEVER AGENCY IS AFFECTING THE SHIP, MY ARMOR SHOWS NO INTERNAL FLUCTUATIONS.
THERE!
CRACK!
CRACK!
IN FACT, I'M BACK TO FULL STRENGTH!
BRAAACK!
NOW FOR DOOM!
CUK
CUK
CUK
CUK
NOT AGAIN!
IT'S OKAY. THEY'RE ON OUR SIDE!
CHUT
CHT CHT
CHUT
I JUST TOLD THEM YOU'RE FRIENDLY.
CHRRT
CHRRT
CHRRT
CHRRT
TOO FRIENDLY.

CONFOUND THESE WRETCHED RODENTS!

FOR EVERY ONE I FLING AWAY, A DOZEN MORE VEX ME!

CUK

CUK

CUK

CUK

CUK

CUK

CUK

CHRT

INTOLERABLE! MY MUCH-VAUNTED TECHNOLOGY-- DECIMATED BY THESE GNAWING RODENTS!
CUK!
CUK!
CUK!
CUK!
CUK!

TIME TO SURRENDER, VON DOOM. YOU'RE ARMOR LOOKS THOROUGHLY DISABLED TO ME.
NEVER!
CUK!
CUK!
CUK
CHRT
BETTER THINK TWICE. I WON'T CALL THEM OFF UNTIL YOU DO!

DOOM WILL NEVER BE DEFEATED! NOT LIKE THIS!
CUK
CUK
CUK
SIC 'IM, GUYS!

CUK!
CUK!
DOOM ALWAYS HAS A FOOLPROOF MEANS OF ESCAPE AT HAND!

MY ARMOR MAY NO LONGER FULLY SERVE ME, THANKS TO THOSE SHARP-TOOTHED PESTS, BUT I AM NOT WITHOUT RESOURCES.
RRRUMMM

DOOM! DON'T BE A FOOL!
GOOD RIDDANCE!
CUK
UNTIL WE MEET AGAIN...
CUK
CUK

CHRRT!
LRRIIP
MY CLOAK!

YOU HAVE NOT HEARD THE LAST OF VICTOR VON DOOM! THIS INDIGNITY SHALL BE AVENGED!

THE DOOMSHIP IS SETTLING. AND THESE WOODS ARE INFESTED WITH VICIOUS RODENTS.
I MUST ESCAPE!
CUK CUK CUK

WATER AHEAD! MY ONLY CHANCE.
CUK CUK
CUK

VICTOR VON DOOM MUST NOT BE VANQUISHED IN THIS IGNOMINIOUS MANNER.
SPLOOSH!

CHRT!

HE SURE STIRRED UP A LOT OF MUD. I DON'T SEE HIM.
HIS BUILT-IN OXYGEN SUPPLY IS LIMITED.
ASSUMING IT'S STILL OPERABLE.

BLOOP!
BLOP!

I DON'T LIKE THE LOOKS OF THAT. I'M GOING IN.
STAY PUT.
SPLASH
DON'T SWEAT IT. SQUIRRELS ARE GREAT SWIMMERS, BUT I'M NOT.

SEALS ARE WORKING. OXYGEN ON.
MY CHEST SEARCHLIGHT SHOULD CUT THROUGH THIS MURK.

THERE'S DOOM'S MASK...

AND THERE HE GOES--BURROWING INTO THE MUD LIKE A CLAM.

NOT SO FAST, DOOM. YOU AND I HAVE UNFINISHED BUSINESS.

NO GOOD! HIS ARMOR'S TOO SLIPPERY--SOME KIND OF SILICON COATING.

MUD. NOTHING BUT MUD.

GOT AWAY, HUH?
AFRAID SO.
SPLASH

SPLOOP!
GUK
GUK

THANKS, MONKEY JOE. GOOD SQUIRREL.
CHRT!

HERE. YOU SHOULD HAVE THIS.
MAYBE THERE ARE SOME NEAT SECRETS INSIDE.
THANKS.

I-I GUESS I KINDA MADE A MESS OF THINGS, HUH?
OH, I DON'T KNOW ABOUT THAT.
YOU MANAGED TO HAND DR. DOOM ONE OF THE MOST INGLORIOUS DEFEATS OF HIS CAREER.

STILL, I'M SO EMBARRASSED. I CAUSED YOU ALL KINDS OF PROBLEMS.

WE MAY NEVER KNOW WHAT HE WAS UP TO, BUT IT'S A CINCH WE SET DOOM'S PLANS BACK--AT LEAST FOR A WHILE.
ALL IN ALL, YOU DID PRETTY WELL.

DOES THAT MEAN YOU'LL TAKE ME ON AS YOUR PARTNER?

OUT OF THE QUESTION. SORRY.
WHAT AM I GOING TO DO? I'M NOT BIG ENOUGH TO GO SUPER HEROING ON MY OWN. AND I CAN'T GO BACK TO SCHOOL.
EVERYBODY CALLS ME "RODENT."

TAKE MY ADVICE. YOU'VE SEEN HOW DANGEROUS THIS BUSINESS IS. TAKE A FEW YEARS OFF. FINISH SCHOOL. GO TO COLLEGE.
IF YOU STILL WANT TO DO THIS AFTER YOU GRADUATE, LOOK ME UP.
YOU MEAN IT! YOU'LL GIVE ME A CHANCE THEN?

WHAT I MEANT WAS I'LL PUT IN A GOOD WORD FOR YOU WITH THE AVENGERS.
I'M NOT BIG ON CROWD SCENES. IF YOU DON'T MIND, I'LL KEEP LOOKING UNTIL I FIND SOMEONE WHO LIKES ME.

I LIKE YOU. HONEST. NO HARD FEELINGS?
WELL... OKAY. IT'S HARD TO STAY MAD AT A GUY IN GLEAMING ARMOR.
GOOD LUCK, SQUIRREL GIRL.

I DON'T NEED LUCK. I EAT NUTS.

"I DON'T NEED LUCK. I EAT NUTS."
THEY'RE NOT GOING TO BELIEVE THIS AT THE NEXT AVENGERS' MEETING.

THE END.

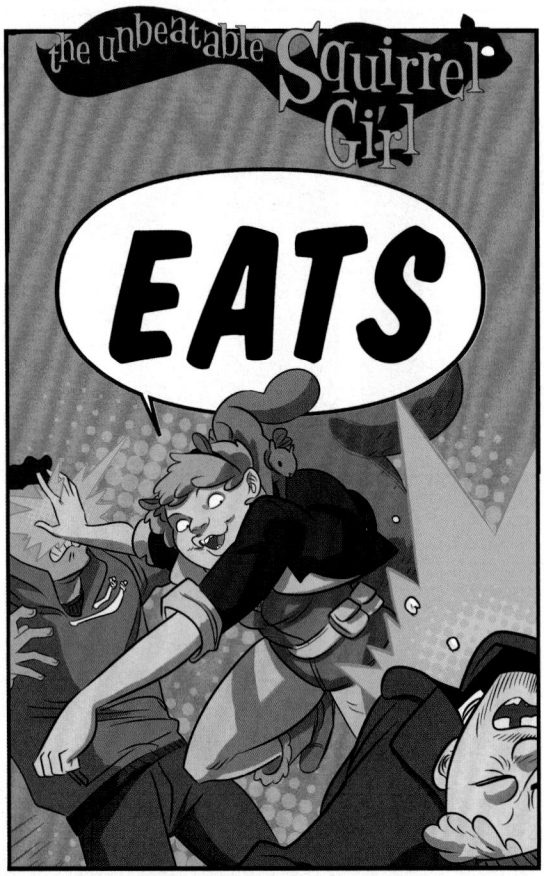

Squirrel Girl is saying "EATS," but what could she be eating? If only there were also a reprinting of issue #2 whose cover clarified this matter in some way!

Oh, Squirrel Girl is eating nuts! Okay, that makes sense. That's really appropriate actually.

What precisely is Squirrel Girl kicking? Is she kicking...butt? Is she kicking...it old school?? The comic MAY be revealed in this issue!

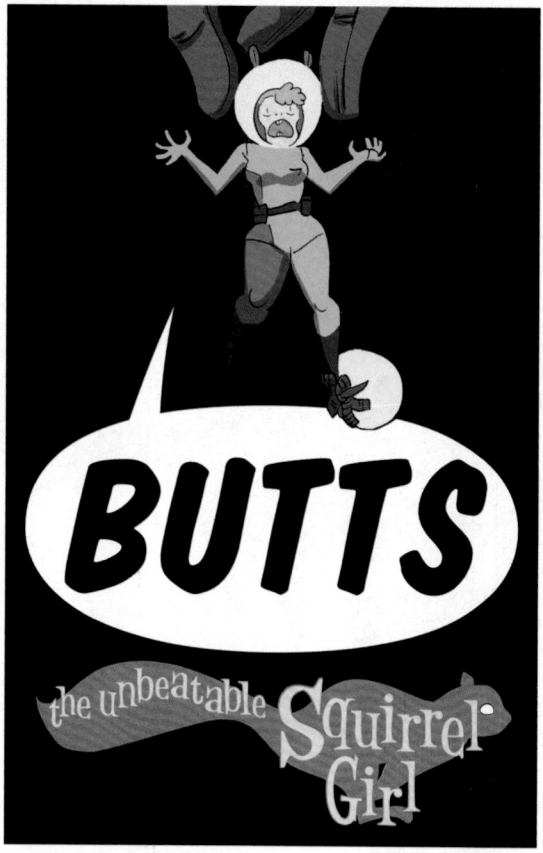

Reader, you hold in your hands the very first Marvel comic whose cover copy is almost 100% comprised of the word "BUTTS." We live in a wonderful time.

I can promise that the situation depicted here on the cover definitely appears in this comic. Far, uh, precisely one panel. Perhaps you are...INTRIGUED??

TOP ROW, FROM LEFT: ISSUE #1 3RD-PRINTING VARIANT COVER, ISSUE #2 3RD-PRINTING VARIANT COVER, ISSUE #3 2ND-PRINTING VARIANT COVER, ISSUE #4 2ND-PRINTING VARIANT COVER.
RIGHT: ISSUE #5 2ND-PRINTING VARIANT COVER

ISSUE #1 VARIANT COVER BY **SKOTTIE YOUNG**